Rev. H. W. Shrewsburry

The Little Lump Of Clay

Rev. H. W. Shrewsburry

The Little Lump Of Clay

ISBN/EAN: 9783743304314

Manufactured in Europe, USA, Canada, Australia, Japa

Cover: Foto ©Thomas Meinert / pixelio.de

Manufactured and distributed by brebook publishing software
(www.brebook.com)

Rev. H. W. Shrewsburry

The Little Lump Of Clay

THE LITTLE LUMP OF CLAY

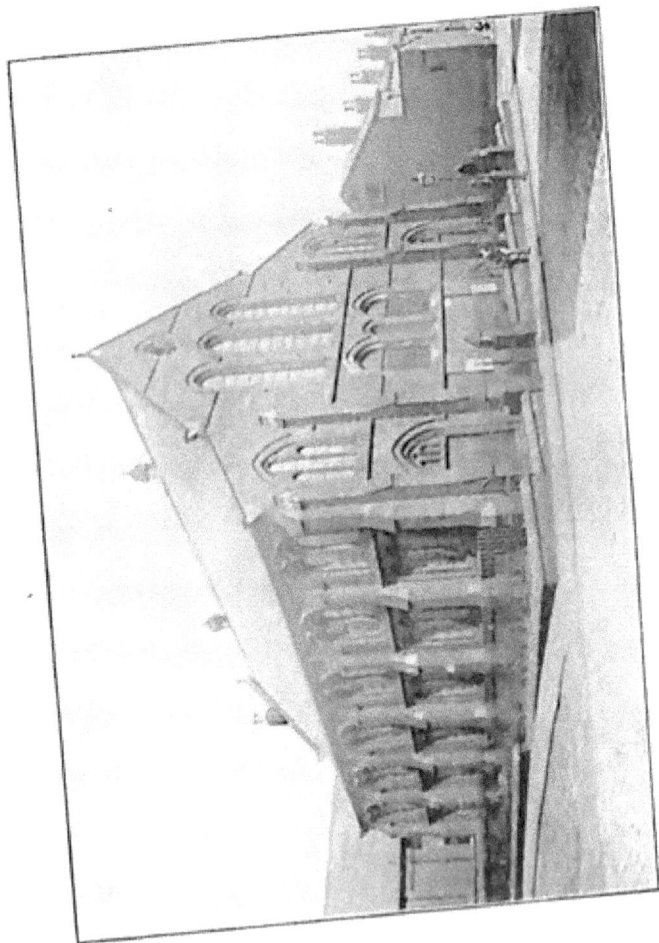

New Wortley Wesleyan Church, Leeds.

THE LITTLE LUMP OF CLAY

AND

Other Addresses to Young People

BY

Rev. H. W. SHREWSBURY

Minister of the New Wortley Wesleyan Church, Leeds

Edinburgh and London

OLIPHANT, ANDERSON & FERRIER

1897

To J. H. B. AND E. B.,

WHOSE LOVE FILLED

MY OWN CHILDHOOD AND BOYHOOD WITH SUNSHINE,

THIS LITTLE BOOK IS AFFECTIONATELY

DEDICATED.

Preface.

THESE Addresses were given in the first
instance to my young friends at New
Wortley, Leeds, on Sabbath mornings.
Usually they were preceded by a Children's Hymn, which the young people
rising in their places sang by themselves,
a feature of the service that always proved
attractive to the adult portion of the con-
gregation.

In each of these addresses the aim has
been to take one central idea and to rivet it
upon the memory. If any of them are
indeed "Golden Nails," and if in any cases
they have been "fastened in sure places,"
to God alone be all the praise.

Subjects.

The Little Lump of Clay.

"What are these?"—REV. vii. 13.

INSTEAD of a sermon, dear young friends, I am going to give you a little tale ; not a true tale, but a tale containing truth,—in other words, a fable.

One day two school lads going home were playing after boys' fashion. One lad took from his pocketful of treasures a little lump of clay. He had broken it off from the mass used for that morning's modelling lesson, and now with a laugh and a " Look out for yourself there ! " he threw it at his companion. The clay

missed its mark, and hitting the plate-
glass window of a jeweller's shop, there it
stuck.   And what an array of beautiful
things the little shapeless lump looked
down upon!   Gold watches, and chains,
and brooches, and bracelets, and all manner
of jewellery.   But just immediately beneath
the clay were three beautiful objects—
three gold rings resting in white satin-
lined cases.   One   ring   contained   a
splendid ruby, and the next a magnificent emerald, and the third a lovely
sapphire.   And as the little lump of
common clay gazed upon these sparkling gems, it swelled with envy and
grief.   The ruby looked as if it had
been born in fire and still retained
its ruddy glow; the emerald like a
crystallised drop of the great ocean;
and the sapphire as if it had dropped
from the deep blue sky.   "Oh!" cried
the clay, "what are these? You beautiful things, how I wish I were one of
you!   But I am so different.   We have
nothing in common."

The jewels looked at one another, and then the emerald flashing a green beam of light spoke up. "Little lump of clay," she said, "you are our own sister. We and you have the same origin. We are only clay in another form."

"That can never be," said the clay, and she was about to argue the point when another boy came by, and picking off the little lump put it in his pocket and hurried away home.

Now this lad's father was a great chemist, and in his laboratory he performed many remarkable experiments. It so happened that that very day he told his wife at dinner how he had been making gems. "What gems?" said she. "Oh, rubies and emeralds and sapphires." The little lump of clay in the lad's pocket began to listen with all its might. "What did you make them of?" the lady inquired. "Out of alumina. You know that's just what common clay is. I crystallised alumina with just a mere trifle of other substances, such as the salts of chromium and cobalt to colour it, and so I made jewels."

"What!" said little seven-year-old Dorothy, "are rubies and emeralds and sapphires made out of nasty, sticky clay?"

"Yes, my little girl," said her father, "that is just about it."

The little lump of clay in the lad's pocket nearly jumped out with joy. "Then," she said to herself, "those beautiful gems were right, and perhaps some day I shall be made like my sisters."

Dear young folk, do you catch the meaning of my little tale? Let us come now to the text. John in his vision saw such bright and beautiful creatures that he was utterly amazed. "What are these?" said the angel to him, and John, quite unable to tell, begged the angel to answer his own question. And the angel's answer was this, those glorious beings were common men and women and common boys and girls transformed. Ah! children, only serve God truly, and you who are now like the little lump of common clay will one day be changed into priceless gems.

But how was it done? you will perhaps ask. How did Dorothy's father make clay into gems? Well, that is a wonderful story, and hard to tell. Dorothy asked, and the little lump of clay heard every word. "My little girl," her father said, " I had to do dreadful things to the poor clay. I had to put it into a crucible and subject it to intense heat. It went through a very fiery trial, I can assure you. But the fire changed it, and the clay became transformed into jewels."

And that was just what the angel told John. These glorious beings were made out of the clay of common human nature, by the tribulations, the fiery trials that is, through which they had come. I don't want you to think, my young friends, that you will have fiery trials just because you are Christians. You will have to pass through tribulations whether you become Christians or not. But there is this difference, the trials of ungodly people are like the heat which bakes clay into common bricks; but the trials of Christ's true followers are like those mysterious forces which transform the clay into beautiful jewels.

An Instance of False Humility.

"We were in our own sight as grasshoppers, and so we were in their sight."—NUM. xiii. 33.

IT is an unfortunate fact that almost all the best things in life have their sham imitations. Sham gold, sham diamonds, sham pearls. There is no end to the shams. And so also it is with the graces of character. The very best of them are counterfeited. There is a sham charity; it is really weak sentiment. There is a sham faith; it is really credulity. And so that rare and beautiful virtue, humility, has been imitated, and in this text we have an instance of a false

humility, which though at first sight it
looks like the genuine thing, is in truth
a base sham, not only useless but positively
mischievous.

Now I could wish few things better for
you, my young friends, than that you
should be " clothed with humility," because
" God resisteth the proud, but giveth grace
to the humble." But I do want to warn
you against that false humility—professed
by some people—which so far from being
pure gold is only Dutch gilt, and beneath
which there is generally to be found the
base metal of cowardice and selfishness.
And therefore I am asking you to listen
to what these men in the text have to say,
and to notice what lies at the bottom of
their pretended humility. Ten of them
have gone from Kadesh, which was meant
to be the last camping - place of the
Israelites in the desert, to spy out the land
of Canaan. They had two duties to per-
form. First to ascertain the best route
of advance, and next to mark carefully
that the land was indeed all that Moses

had described it, and to bring back their witness to that fact for the encouragement of the people. And now that they have returned they all agree as to the beauty and fruitfulness of the land, and two of them, Joshua and Caleb, give counsel to go up at once, and possess it. But Shammua and Shaphat and their six companions declare the thing impossible. The cities were too strong to be taken, and the people were such giants, that said they, " We were in our own sight as grasshoppers, and so we were in their sight." The fact is these men saw that there was some hard fighting to be done. And they were too cowardly to face it. They did not like to say we daren't fight, or we won't fight. That was what they meant, but what they said was that they were so puny and feeble in comparison with their enemies that it would be useless to fight. Now, how do you suppose Shammua and Shaphat and the rest would have liked it, if just when they were about to start upon their expedition Moses had said, " We can't allow these

B

men to go, they are no better than grasshoppers. Choose some others in their
stead"? Can't you imagine how angry
they would have been, and how they
would have boasted that Moses couldn't
find any fitter men for the task in all the
camp? Ah! my young friends, you will
find that this very old game, of professing
to be something we shouldn't like any one
else to call us, is still played when men
want to escape some disagreeable duty.
Sometimes a man is asked to give to some
good cause, and he replies, " I really can't
afford to. You have no idea how badly
off I am." But suppose some one set
the report going, " Mr X—— can't afford
to take his family to the sea-side this year.
He's dreadfully poor, you know," how
angry Mr X—— would be, and how ready
to declare that he had a bigger balance at
the bank than some people who made a
great deal more show. Or Mr Z—— is
asked to undertake some office in the
church which will require much time and
care. He does not like to say he is un-

willing to make the sacrifice. So he says, "You must please excuse me, I really have not talent enough for so responsible a position." But if when Mr Z——'s name was suggested for some position, any one should say, "Oh, it's no good asking Mr Z——, he's not equal to that," how vexed he would be. It was all false humility put on to escape some self-denial.

Don't take up with this sham, my young friends. Guard against it now in little things. Don't say you are no good at cricket, you would only spoil the game, when what you really want is to be left in peace just now to finish that story-book. Don't say you can't run a hem fit to be seen, when what you really mean is, you would rather be off for a stroll with another of your companions than stop and help this one with her work. And remember it is better to have tried and failed than never to have tried at all.

And now I want you to notice what the false humility of these eight men did.

First, it dishonoured God. There would

have been no great harm in the men
saying that they were as grasshoppers in
their own sight, but there *was* harm in
adding, "and so we were in their sight."
Because these men were in some sense
God's representatives, and in thus belittling
themselves in comparison with their
enemies, they belittled God. When an
ambassador goes to a foreign court, though
personally he may be the most modest
and retiring of men, yet for his monarch's
and country's sake he will magnify his
office, and insist on all respect being
shown to him. There are times when true
humility shows itself in splendid boasting.
It was true humility that led the youthful
David to boast to Goliath, " Thou comest
to me with a sword and with a spear and
with a shield : but I come to thee in the
name of the Lord of hosts, the God of the
armies of Israel, whom thou hast defied.
This day will the Lord deliver thee into
mine hand ; and I will smite thee, and
take thine head from thee." How much
better was that than if David had said :

" I dare not fight this giant ; I am only a grasshopper in his sight." And so again it was true humility when Paul boasted splendidly, " I can do all things through Christ which strengtheneth me." Dear young friends, you have your giants to fight—temper, and pride, and sloth, and selfishness, and many more. Don't say you are only grasshoppers, and you cannot fight them. That dishonours God. Say rather that you can fight them, and will fight them, and that in the name of Jesus Christ you will overthrow them. For even if you are as grasshoppers, what then? Grasshoppers with God behind them are more than a match for giants.

In the second place this false humility discouraged the people. They were so much distressed by the spies' report that they all wept, and then set up a clamour to go straight back to Egypt. For cowardice is an infectious disease and spreads rapidly. I heard a boy say one day, " It's no good trying, I can't conquer my bad temper." That lad had a good

home, and good parents, and everything
to help him. Just think how discouraging
that would have been to any lads who had
no good homes or kind friends. I want
you, my young friends, to be brave and
strong not only for your own sakes, but
because if you are not, you will discourage
so many others where you might help
them.

In the third place this false humility
resulted in death to the men themselves.
A plague fell upon them, and they died.
They were afraid of the men of Canaan,
but they forgot that they had to reckon
with the Lord, and the sickness which
swept them away is set down as God's
judgment upon their cowardice and un-
belief. How much better to have died
bravely on the battle-field than thus to
perish miserably in the camp! But they
would not have died in battle. God had
promised them victory, and if they had
trusted Him, they would have had it. This
is a very solemn lesson. I do beg you to
remember you must either fight or perish.

There are hundreds of boys and girls who have lost everything because they were too cowardly to fight the giants. Do not let it be so in your case, my young friends. Do not call yourselves grasshoppers. Call yourselves God's heroes and heroines, and go forth in His strength to win many a splendid victory over sin, self, and Satan.

A Happy Removal.

"Wells digged, which thou diggedst not."—
DEUT. vi. 11.

WHEN we are trying to describe the character of people we sometimes give a hint at it by telling the name of the quarter in which they live. Sometimes we say they live in Praise Street, or in Contentment Place, or in Happiness Square, and you know at once what is meant, that they are people of a thankful or contented or happy disposition. Praise Street is a beautiful street to dwell in, but unfortunately there are always a great many houses to let in it. But there is one street, and it is a very long one,

which is always full. It is called Grumbling
Street, and there is this peculiarity about
it, the houses all face the north and scarcely
get any sunshine. But every house has a
well in the garden. Some of these wells
are full of sweet pure water, and some are
choked up with rubbish. And the people
pay nothing for the water. But they never
think of that. Indeed, often they have a
strange idea that they made the wells
themselves, and that they have a perfect
right to the water. Which is quite a
delusion, for the wells were there long
before the people became tenants of the
houses. Now it is all due to those wells
that people ever get out of Grumbling
Street. And when they have got out of it,
and found a place in some brighter neighbourhood, they always speak of the change
as their happy removal. It comes about
in this way. Sometimes a tenant in
Grumbling Street begins to think, " I
wonder who dug that well in my garden,"
and then he goes on to reflect, " it has been
a very good thing for me," and so soon as

ever he feels that he begins to see what a gloomy street he has been dwelling in, and he moves on into the next street, which is called *Better Fashion Street*, and if he be a truly wise man, he will not stop there long, but he will move again, until he finds himself at length in one of the roomy and sunny mansions in the beautiful street called Praise.

My dear young friends, when God opens our blind eyes we see clearly how many blessings we have which we neither deserved nor worked for, what wells of sweet water we are daily drinking from which we never dug. And to realise this makes us ashamed of murmuring and dis-content, and we begin to grow thankful and happy and anxious to be worthy of our blessings.

There was once a man shut up in a dingy prison cell for some political offence. He was very miserable and very angry and very despairing. But one day a little bit of green appeared in a crevice between the paving-stones of his cell floor. It had sprung up from a seed that had wafted in, and it grew into a tender shoot, and the prisoner cared for it, and shared with it his daily allowance of water. It became a companion to him, such as the gourd tree was to Jonah sitting in angry loneliness watching for the destruction of Nineveh.

And it put new thoughts into the prisoner's mind. Surely, he said to himself, God has not quite forgotten me. And so his gloom and anger and despair passed away, and he became cheerful and hopeful, and was able to bear up bravely until his long imprisonment was over.

There are times, I daresay, when you feel sad or discontented, or out of heart; at such times the best remedy is to think what wells you have which you never dug, what blessings have come into your life, not through your own merit or work, but by the toil and sufferings of those who have gone before you. Let me point out a few of these wells.

To begin with, there is the *Well of Liberty*. You are living in a free land.

You cannot be bought or sold as children are in some countries. You can go to God's house as often as you like. You can read God's Word when you will. It was not always so. There was a time when you could not have read your Bible, if you had had money enough to possess one, and learning enough to understand it, which most probably you would not have had, without running a terrible risk of being imprisoned or even put to death. And this liberty has been secured for you at the cost of the lives of many brave men and women. They dug the well, and you enjoy its sweet waters.

Then there is the *Well of Education.* You boys and girls of twelve years old have been taught more in these days than your great-grandfathers could learn in all their lifetime. How they would have prized the opportunities which are yours for nothing. If you could only realise how in their days they thirsted for knowledge, and thirsted in vain, you would indeed thank God for this well which has been dug for you, and you would drink deep draughts from it.

Again, there is the *Well of Health.* Do you ever think how much care and thought have been bestowed upon you to ensure your growing up strong and hearty? How your fathers have toiled to earn a sufficiency of food and clothing for you, how your mothers have watched by you through infant diseases, and nursed you into strength? How many crippled and suffering boys and girls there are to-day that you would be like if kind hands had not dug for you this well of health.

And best of all there is the *Well of Love.* What a deep, inexhaustible well is that! The love of God first, the love of parents next, the love of friends and companions. What have you done to make that well? Nothing. It was there, already dug, when you were born, and if every other well failed you, you could still lead a happy life with this well to draw from.

Think of these wells, my young friends, and many others besides, wells made ready to hand for you without any effort on your part. And if ever you find yourselves living in the dark and cheerless Grumbling Street, the remembrance of all these mercies will cause you quickly to change your abode, and that will be both for you and for others a happy removal.

The Prophet's Little Cake.

"Make me thereof a little cake first."—1 KINGS xvii. 13.

NOW, doesn't that sound a selfish request for a preacher to make? Here was a poor widow, a perfect stranger to Elijah, and when the prophet has heard from her own lips that she has a mere handful of meal, and a few drops of oil, just enough to make a cake to share between herself and her son, and after that, nothing, he actually tells her to go and light her bit of fire and make him a little cake first. For him first! and then what would there be left for herself and her son?

Certainly it does seem at first sight a most extraordinarily bold and selfish thing to ask, and especially for a prophet of the Lord to ask, a man who should set an example in all that is beautiful and unselfish.

But the fact is, when Elijah asked to have a cake made for himself first, he spoke not as a beggar but as a prophet. It mattered nothing to him personally whether the woman granted his request or refused it. He knew that he was perfectly safe. For God who had already made the ravens His servants could easily find some other way of supplying his need if this woman declined to help him. But it mattered a great deal to the woman. Because Elijah followed up his request with a splendid promise of what God was prepared to do for her. Now, suppose she had persisted in her refusal. Suppose she had been suspicious, and said, "This is a fine tale you tell me, but I'm not going to be so simple as to believe it," what would have

happened? She would have baked her
last cake, and when she and her son
had eaten it, because there was nothing
else left in the house, and she had not
money with which to buy provisions at
famine prices, she and her son after that
last meal would have starved to death.
But the woman believed that God spoke
through Elijah, and she took God at His
word, and the result was that all through
those terrible days, when people on every
side were perishing of hunger, the woman
found she had sufficient in the house to
keep herself and her son and Elijah
alive.

This is an old story, I know, and a
very wonderful one, so wonderful that
some people, I daresay, don't believe it.
But I want to impress upon you, my
young friends, that this same experience
is being repeated every day in the lives
of many people, and in ways not less
wonderful. God's promise is the same in
all ages, that where His people honour
Him with their trust, He will honour

them with His protection. But they
must not demand that God shall fill the
barrel with meal and the cruise with oil
first, and that then they will make His
prophet a little cake. They must be
ready, if God requires it, to give away
their last crust, their last penny, and to
believe that when they are absolutely
reduced to nothing God will provide for
them. And that is just what some people
will not do. They have not faith enough
in God to do it.

I used to know a woman who kept a
little shop next door to a chapel. It
was open all the week through, and on
Sundays many of the Sunday scholars
would stand looking at the sweets in the
window, and then yielding to temptation
would go in and buy. She was a hard-
working, industrious woman, and she had
a sick husband to provide for. When I
spoke to her about the matter, and pointed
out that she was not only throwing away
God's gift of Sabbath rest, but leading
the young folk into Sabbath breaking,

she owned at once that it was wrong. She had not been brought up to that sort of thing, she said, and she did not like it. She could not herself attend God's house under the circumstances, because she felt it would be hypocritical. But then, she pleaded, she made her rent by Sunday trading, and she really could not give it up until an equal sum was provided in some other way. You see she wanted God to fill the barrel before she made the little cake. She had not faith in God, and dare not make the little cake first.

On the other hand, a good man once told me that from the time he shut up his shop on Sundays his business had increased wonderfully. And you will find that this is the general testimony of good people. They will tell you over and over again that Jesus Christ's promise has come true, "Seek ye first the kingdom of God and His righteousness, and all these things shall be added unto you." Now let me beg of you, my young friends, to prove

what I say in this easy manner. Ask
right and left of Christian people you
know, or meet casually, this question,
"Were you ever the worse for giving up
anything for God? Did anything ever
happen in your life like the experience of
the widow woman of Zarephath?" If you
ask these questions often enough, you are
sure to meet with some remarkable life
stories, wonderful accounts of men and
women who having been brought to the
very verge of starvation for conscience'
sake have been lifted into positions of
ease and comfort. I might give you
some examples, but it will be much more
interesting to you, and do you much more
good, to find out illustrations for yourselves.

And Jesus Christ has made it plain to
us *why* this is so. You remember that on
one occasion the devil suggested to Jesus
Christ to stay His hunger by making
bread for Himself out of stones. It would
have been a dreadful thing for reasons I
must not stop to explain, if Jesus Christ

had done that.   He replied, " Man shall
not live by bread alone."   So that there
is something else we may depend upon
when bread fails.   What can it be ?   " But
by every word which proceedeth out of
the mouth of God."   Now what does that
mean ?   Let us see.   When the children
of Israel were passing through the wilderness their bread failed.   God spoke a
word, and the manna came.   In the days
of famine Elijah's bread failed.   God spoke
a word, and the ravens came.   This widow
woman's bread failed.   God spoke a word,
and every day meal and oil came.   Jesus
Christ's bread failed.   God spoke a word,
and as soon as the devil was clean gone,
" behold, angels came and ministered unto
him."   And so all along God's people
have found that when their supplies
have failed, failed because they were true
to God and to their duty, one word from
God was enough, and in the most unexpected way and through the most un-
looked for sources, help came to them.

Now, to finish this little talk, I want to

urge upon you that *poverty*, poverty of
any kind, is the worst possible excuse you
can make for refusing to do God service.
People often say, We can't give, we are
too poor ; we can't undertake this duty,
we are too weak, or too ignorant.   My
dear young friends, it is a terrible mistake, a truly fatal blunder.   If you are
short of money, or short of brains, or
short of anything, the greater the reason
that out of your poverty you should do
something for God.   Refuse, and you lose
everything.   Have faith to make for
God the little cake first, and in ways
you would never dream of He will enrich
your life, and turn your poverty into
plenty.

Wrong Labels on the Bottles.

"He called it Nehushtan."—2 KINGS xviii. 4.

LET us put this into plain English, as it is given in the margin of your Bibles. "And he called it a piece of brass." What a common name is this to give to a very old, very precious, and very interesting relic! Right down through seven hundred years to the days of King Hezekiah there had been carefully preserved that famous brazen serpent which Moses erected in the wilderness for the cure of the Israelites bitten by venomous snakes. It was one of the few objects that remained as memorials to the people of

those far distant days when their fathers
journeyed through the desert to the land of
Promise.   It was indeed a very remarkable
relic, but the people had made an idol of it,
and therefore the good king, much as it
must have grieved him, had it broken up,
and gave it a nickname.   Imagine any one
calling that ancient stone beneath the
Queen's coronation chair, on which Jacob
is said to have laid his head at Bethel, a
lump of rock!   And yet if we were foolish
enough to worship the stone, and to burn
incense to it, as a god, such a nickname
would be well deserved.   It would remind
us that the thing we were wickedly making
into an idol was only a bit of common
material; and notwithstanding its age and
its intensely interesting associations, it
would be better for it to be destroyed than
that it should cause the nation to fall into
a senseless superstition.

Now I want you, my young friends, to
open your eyes to the fact that there are a
great many things tolerated about which
we should feel very uncomfortable if only

we gave some such plain name to them as Hezekiah gave to this idolised brazen serpent. Just think what would happen if in a chemist's shop the wrong names and labels were upon the bottles and drawers. If for instance spirits of salts were in a sweet nitre bottle, or laudanum in a cough-mixture bottle, or magnesia in the white-lead drawer, and so on. Before the mistakes were found out there might be some very awkward results. Well, in the great shop we call the world, there has been a good deal of tampering with the labels, and there is great need that now and again some Hezekiah should set to work boldly to put matters straight and give things their proper names.

Let us give you an illustration or two of what I mean. A party of young men go off with their friends for a country jaunt. A long drive in waggonettes, tea at a public-house or restaurant, and plenty of foolish jesting. Now what do they call it? They say it is RECREATION. That sounds well, doesn't it? It seems such a simple innocent thing under that label. But Hezekiah would call it SABBATH BREAK-ING. And that gives it quite another look. But you may say, Isn't the Sabbath a day for recreation? It is indeed ; for recreation of this sort, "They that wait upon the Lord shall renew their strength." Your fathers and grandfathers worked long hours and had few holidays, while to-day there are shorter hours and many holidays. Yet they kept the Sabbath far more sacredly as a day for waiting upon God. Shame upon us if with vastly more leisure time we rob God, and rob our own souls of the day of worship. When on the Lord's Day your recreation is of a kind, however harmless, that puts Him, and His service, and His house, and His Word, out of mind, label the bottle POISON—SABBATH-BREAKING.

As you grow older you will find that there is one most useful label. It serves to disguise the real nature of many sins. It reads in one word—BUSINESS. Sharp practice on 'Change, tricks of trade, one-sided bargains, all made respectable by this innocent-looking term. Hezekiah's labels would have been *Gambling* and *Cheating*.

Perhaps there is a little tea-party, and tongues are going fast, and all the talk is of the faults of one and the weaknesses of another. There is a beautiful label for this. It goes by the name of SOCIAL INTER-COURSE. I think Hezekiah would have called it *a backbiting banquet.*

And so the thing goes on. All round the wrong names are exhibited, "fibs" for "lies," "independence" for "rudeness," "prudence" for "selfishness," "charity beginning at home" for "love of money," "religion" for "serving God and mammon." And so many a soul has been poisoned because of the wrong labels on the bottles.

Dear young people, be like Hezekiah in this matter of calling things by their true names. Don't suppose a little sin ceases to be sin because it is a little one. The tiniest twig on an oak tree is as truly oak wood as the largest bough. And the smallest deception is as truly a lie as the most massive falsehood. If you will read often and carefully Jesus Christ's sermon on the mount, it will keep your moral judgment clear, and you will soon learn how to label things correctly. And it will help you wonderfully to live true, and honest, and beautiful lives. When you have acquired this habit of giving to every kind of conduct its proper name, you will have the joy then of knowing you are true disciples of the Lord Jesus Christ, who hated shams, and the cloaking of evil things under pleasant sounding names.

The Western Gate.

'At Parbar westward, four at the causeway, and two at Parbar."—1 CHRON. xxvi. 18.

I HAVE been asked to give an address from this text. What the motive was that prompted the request we will not inquire. Thomas Fuller, the most remarkable preacher of his day, once heard the text given out, " Am not I thine ass upon which thou hast ridden ever since I was thine unto this day? Was I ever wont to do so unto thee?" To his surprise from that queer text the preacher drew some very useful lessons, which led Fuller to remark, " How fruitful are the seeming barren places of Scripture. Bad plough- men which make balks [uneven places between the furrows] of such ground. Wheresoever the surface of God's Word doth not laugh and sing with corn, there the heart thereof within is merry with mines, affording, where not plain matter, hidden mysteries." Let us see then if from this odd-sounding text in the First Book of Chronicles we cannot gather some beautiful thought to treasure up.

The first part of this chapter deals with the doorkeepers appointed to guard the entrances to the temple, the positions given to them, and the number stationed at each gate. So many for the doors on the north, so many for the south, so many for east and west. And it is in regard to one of the entrances on the west side of the temple that this text occurs, "At Parbar westward, four at the causeway, and two at Parbar." There are two words in this text which, if we quite knew their meaning, would make the whole passage perfectly plain. One of these words, *Parbar*, is a Hebrew term, which the translator has left untouched because its meaning was so uncertain. The other word, *causeway*, means a high road, probably some special approach to the temple. Now if you will look at a map of Jerusalem, you will notice that running along the whole of the western side of the temple there is a valley, and across the valley the hill of Zion. On Mount Zion stood the royal palace, and from hill to hill, across the mighty ravine known as the Tyropœon Valley, there stretched an ascent, or causeway, or viaduct, a royal road uniting palace and temple. Traces of such a viaduct may be seen in Jerusalem to-day, and it is a possible conjecture that this mighty bridge which once spanned the valley, was the "ascent" mentioned in 1 Kings x. 5, and the "causeway" of this text.

The word *Parbar* seems to mean a portico or arched gateway, or perhaps some building from which this entrance took its name. So that, giving these meanings to the words used in the text, and filling it out a little, it would read something like this:—"At the western gate six doorkeepers, namely four for the royal viaduct and two for the gate."

What I want you then to keep in mind is this, that, according to our supposition, the western gate was the royal approach to the temple. There were many other entrances; through them the common people passed—the sick, the sad, the sinful. But the western gate was the king's gate, and here at least you may be sure the doorkeepers were always on the lookout, that whenever the king came they might open to him immediately.

And now, my young friends, the lesson comes in that I should like to impress upon you from the text. The Apostle Paul describes our bodies as "temples of the Holy Ghost," and these temples have many gates. John Bunyan, in his "Holy War,"—a book I would have you all read, —calls them Eyegate, Eargate, Nosegate, Mouthgate, Feelgate. These gates are ever open, and by means of them we are in constant communication with the world.

Through these approaches worldly thoughts, worldly desires, worldly ambitions, worldly pleasures, worldly cares, are continually thronging in upon us. *What about the western gate?* Is there no royal viaduct to bridge the gulf that separates us from heaven? Is there no royal portico by which the Lord our King may visit His temple? Thank God there is. Jesus Christ says, " I am the way "; and the more earnestly you study His life and teaching, the more clearly you will understand that He is the viaduct across the otherwise impassable chasm that stretches between men and God. I do not know who may be the doorkeepers on the farther side of that viaduct where it touches the better life, but on this side I think they are Faith and Hope, and the doorkeepers at the western gate itself are surely Prayer and Praise. But what if Prayer be dead, and Praise absent? Then the gate remains fast barred, and the King cannot bring into His temple the glory and brightness of His presence. Oh, my young friends,

D

how I wish I could make you realise that
all that is noblest, all that is purest, all that
is most beautiful and joyous, can only
come into your life by this royal approach.
It is not the books that you read, nor the
sermons that you hear, that will make you
great and glad, but the moments you
spend upon your knees thanking God from
the depth of your heart for His loving-
kindness, and praying Him earnestly to
lead you into all truth and goodness.

If I were to ask, When should the
western gate be opened? I daresay many
of you would answer twice a day, at the
time of morning and evening prayer. But
surely that must be a mistaken notion.
The other gates are open all the day long.
Why should we give God fewer opportunities of coming to us than we give the
world? It seems to me that this gate
should be like the gates of that city
described in Isaiah (chapter lx. 11): "Thy
gates shall be open continually : they shall
not be shut day nor night." And so it
has been with many good men, to whom

the Lord has revealed Himself not only
in their waking thoughts, but in visions of
the night also. This is what is called
praying without ceasing. It does not
mean that you should always be upon
your knees. That of course would be
impossible. It does not even mean that
you should always be thinking about God.
What it does mean is this—that you
should live always in a thankful spirit, and
that you should so be lifted above sin and
selfishness, that at all times your minds
will be open to the beautiful thoughts, and
sweet influences, and noble aims, which
not only at morning and evening prayer
time, but all the day through, yes, and in
your dreams also, God is ever ready to
give you.

And now I hope I have made my lesson
plain. Right over against the temple of
your soul is the palace of your King.
Dear young people, *keep the western gate
always open.*

A Lover of Worms.

"Man that is a worm."—JOB xxv. 6.

THERE it lay upon the top step of
the path leading into the recreation ground, stretching out its
whole length of four inches and basking in
the spring sunshine,—there it lay, a plump
live earthworm, little heeding that it ran a
terrible risk of being trodden underfoot
any minute. Now it so happened that as
we—nine-year-old Jack, and seven-year-old
Kathie, and Father—came to the spot
intent on a romp together that Saturday
morning, the little folk, whose every
sentence took the form of a question, were
asking, "What are you going to preach to

the children about to-morrow morning?"
And there was the answer right before us.
I picked the little fellow up, displayed his
ringed framework, threw him gently on the
nearest bed out of harm's way, and replied,
"We will have a sermon on worms."
"What!" cried boy and girl together, "is
there a text in the Bible about worms?"
And the very idea tickled their fancy.

Now there is such a text, my young
friends, and here it is. Bildad is speaking.
He has come to comfort Job in his afflic-
tion, and like many other would-be
comforters, who are prompted by duty
rather than by love, the crumbs of comfort
he offers are more likely to choke the poor
sufferer than to nourish him. It is a
strange way that some people have of
comforting their friends by telling them
their misfortunes are due to their own
faults, or that their troubles are not half as
bad as they might have been. "Ah!" says
a neighbour to the sad mother who is
weeping for her baby snatched away by
scarlet fever, "you ought to be very thank-

ful your Mary wasn't took as well." Such a comforter was Bildad, and in this particular passage he is telling Job that men are but as worms to God, and that Job ought to be grateful God had not set His foot upon him and trampled him out of existence. Now Bildad was quite right when he declared that as compared to the great, and mighty, and all-knowing God, a man is but as a worm. But he quite forgot that God is a lover of worms, and that He would not recklessly inflict pain upon the meanest creature.

I fear there are some men who would not turn aside a hair's breadth to spare a worm. They would crush it underfoot if it lay in their path, or chop it in half with the spade if they turned one up in digging in their garden. But there are some men who are not so, and there is one man who above all others deserves to be called the friend of earthworms, I mean the great naturalist Charles Darwin. He found in worms a subject worthy of close study. He devoted time and patience to finding out how they are fashioned and what they do, and then he wrote a book about them, a book which some day I hope you will read, and by reading which I hope you will learn to admire the beautiful spirit of the author. And in that book Charles Darwin has glorified the common earthworm. He has taught the world that the worm is one of God's busiest workers and one of man's best friends. These untiring toilers are in truth living ploughs, and with ceaseless industry they are constantly engaged in turning up the earth, and so making it soft and fit to receive the countless millions of seeds that are strewn on it.

Now whilst Bildad reminds us that men are but worms, I want to remind you that just as Darwin was a lover of worms, God is a lover of men. He will not ruthlessly trample upon them and hurt and crush them, and if at times He permits them to be tempted and troubled, it is only that He may in His wisdom and goodness make "all things work together for good" for them that love Him.

In order to give you an idea of how much God loves and cares for men, I am going to suppose a very wonderful and impossible thing.

Imagine—for you young people are clever at imagining—imagine that Charles Darwin had gone to some magician and spoken to him after this fashion. "My friend, I am studying earthworms. I want to know all about them. I have watched them many a long day, but that is not enough for me. I want to live with them, and work amongst them as they work. In fact I want to be a worm. I pray you, therefore, touch me with your magic wand and turn me into an earthworm." And imagine that thereupon the magician had stretched forth his wand and touched the great naturalist and transformed him into a worm, and that for months and years Charles Darwin had burrowed in the earth, living as worms live, and toiling as worms toil, and that at length when thus as one of themselves he had found out everything about them, by a second touch of the

magician's wand he had been turned back
again into a man. What would you say
to that? Would you not say it was a very
convincing proof that the naturalist had
the very deepest interest in worms, and
that after that he could never wilfully
injure one?

My dear young friends, this seems to
you, I daresay, a tremendous stretch of
imagination. Yet that is precisely what
God has done for "man that is a worm."
Listen to what the Bible says, "Have this
mind in you which was also in Christ
Jesus: who being in the form of God,
counted it not a prize to be on an equality
with God, but emptied Himself, taking the
form of a servant, being made in the like-
ness of men" (Phil. ii. 6, 7). And again:
"Since then the children are sharers in
flesh and blood, He also Himself in like
manner partook of the same" (Heb. ii. 14).
And now, whenever next you see a lowly
worm crossing your path, remember that
whilst Bildad teaches us that in comparison
with God we are just as insignificant,

Jesus Christ teaches us that He, though equal with God, became actually one of us, because He is a lover of worms, and because He wants to raise us, worms of earth as we are, to the glory of His own heavenly life.   Think of all that this means, and try, dear children, to be worthy of this wonderful love God has for you.

Good out of Evil.

" An instrument of ten strings."—Ps. xxxiii. 2.

THE instrument mentioned in this text is the *nebel* or ten-stringed harp.

Now, did it ever occur to you, my young friends, to ask how men came to make harps, and to bring forth beautiful music from them? Did it ever occur to you when you have listened to some one playing, say one of Beethoven's wonderful sonatas, upon your beautiful new piano, with its iron frame, and check action, and rich ringing chords, to ask yourself the question. "I wonder what was the very beginning of a piano?" You remember

quite well, it may be, your old piano, and
how different it was from this one, in touch
and tone; and it is just possible that
when you were teasing for the new piano
you heard your grandmother say that she
thought the old one good enough, that
she remembered in her grandmother's
time it would have been considered a very
remarkable instrument indeed, for they had
no pianoforte then, only the harpsichord,
which was a much simpler sort of thing;
and before that were the spinet and
virginal, and before these the clavicord
and clavicytherium; and before them the
dulcimer, which was little more than a set
of strings mounted on a sounding box.
And so, if you went back in the history of
the piano, you would come at length to
the ten-stringed harp of this text, and find
in it a remote ancestor of the beautiful
modern instrument that stands in your
drawing-room. But still we have not got
to the very beginning. For though this
ten-stringed harp is almost a toy compared
to your piano at home, it was nevertheless

a fine instrument, and upon it in the grand
services of the temple where these psalms
were sung the harpers played their accom-
paniments. Indeed, the origin of the harp
belongs to those far distant ages of which
we know so little, but I think we may
make a shrewd guess at it. Before the
ten-stringed harp there was a three-stringed
harp, and you will say then before the
three-stringed harp was there a one-stringed
harp? There was, and when I remind you
that before men began to *sing* and *play*
they began to *hunt* and to *fight*, you will
judge at once that that one-stringed harp
was nothing else than a *bow*. The likeli-
hood is that in those beginnings of history
when might was right, and every man
depended upon his weapon, that one day
some warrior plucking his bow-string in
an idle moment was struck with its musical
twang. That next he observed the note
altered according to the extent to which
the string was stretched. Then two, three,
or more strings would be tried, next a
sounding-board was added, and so the

harp came into existence. And thus was fulfilled that beautiful saying, "Thou makest the wrath of men to praise Thee;" and so God brought good out of evil, when the bow, the weapon of death, suggested those sweet toned harps, to the music of which the songs of the psalmists were sung, and from those harps again, the instrument of ten strings having grown into an instrument of eighty-five strings, come the pianos of to-day, to which you sing your hymns of Christian praise. If this indeed is the true history of the harp, as there is reason for believing, is it not indeed a fine example of good out of evil?

Now let us carry this thought a little further. There are certain things in character which may be either bow-strings for the devil to make mischief with, or harp-strings for God to make music with. You may think it a strange thing to say, but your highest hopes lie in your worst faults. You are plagued I daresay, every one of you, with what is called a "besetting sin." Some of you find it so hard to

restrain your bad temper, some of you not
to be selfish, or lazy, or sullen, or cowardly,
or deceitful. Now what is a besetting sin?
It is really some distinctive feature in your
character put to a wrong use, something
which if rightly tuned and touched would
be of the greatest value. A besetting sin
means that there is something in you of
which the Evil One is making a bow-string,
but which God, if you will let Him, will
turn into a harp-string.

For instance, mother says, " I don't know
what to do with our Dick. He is so self-
willed I cannot manage him at all." So
Dick's besetting sin, it seems, is obstinacy.
But one day a beautiful thing happens to
Dick. He feels that he has often been a
bad lad, and he wants to be a good one.
He gets down upon his knees and asks
God to forgive him, and help him to do
better, and to make him a true follower of
Jesus Christ. And as he grows up into a
young man he is always trying to do the
right, and praying every day for God's
help. And now Dick has become a fine

six-foot young fellow engaged in a large
business house. What about the old
obstinacy? It is still there, but it has
taken another form. Hear what Dick's
master has to say, "There isn't any one in
my employ I would trust sooner than Dick.
He always sticks to his principles." So you
see the bow-string has become a harp-
string, and God has brought good out of
evil.

And so, my young friends, it will always be. If you are trying to live for
God, those faults which have so much
discouraged you yourselves, and caused your
friends so much pain, will be transformed
into the finest features of your character.
The Apostle John was by nature a fiery-
tempered man, a son of thunder; after his
conversion that fiery temper became holy
zeal for God. The Apostle Peter was by
nature a rash, impulsive man; after his
conversion that rashness became a holy
boldness for Christ. The Apostle James
was by nature a suspicious, unbelieving
man; after his conversion that suspicion

became holy caution, and fitted him above the other apostles to guide the infant Church through the perils of its early years. In each case God took the devil's bow-string, and turned it into a harp-string to sound only for His praise. Do not therefore be discouraged about your be-setting sins. Only give yourselves fully to God, and in your character He will bring forth good out of evil.

There is just one other thing I want to say to you about this text. It speaks of an instrument of *ten* strings. The more strings the richer the music. I have heard a tune fiddled out on *one* string only of a violin. It was interesting and clever, but it was not exactly music. Dear young people, let your character be like a ten-stringed harp at least. Let there be a beautiful variety of good qualities in it. There are some people who seem to think that if they are just and true and upright, nothing more is needed. But the music of such lives lacks richness and sweetness. In his letter to the Churches the Apostle

E

Paul speaks not only of love and faith and truth, the chief strings in the harp of character, but of many other virtues besides; of being kindly affectioned, pitiful, courteous, patient, sympathetic, forgiving, and considerate. There are ten strings, and if they all be found in your character, and God's fingers touch them, the music of your life will be very sweet indeed, and long after it has ceased on earth the memory of it will be precious.

A Coloured Diary.

"The days of thy youth."—ECCLES. xii. 1.

"WAYWARD TOM,"—that was his mother's name for him; other people called him "that disagreeable lad." He was indeed a sad scapegrace, twelve years old in age, and quite fifteen in mischief. Not that he was really bad at heart. He liked good people, and he liked to be good himself when it cost him no trouble. But self was always first with Tom. It mattered nothing to him that he vexed his father and grieved his mother, and made himself a nuisance to his friends, so long as he could get his own way and please himself. So never a day passed but Tom was in trouble. No lad got the cane more frequently at school, or was oftener in disgrace at home. Tom's mother mourned in secret, and asked the Lord what would become of her boy if all the days of his youth passed thus. But secret sighs and tears would never cure Tom. That his mother knew well, and being a quick-witted woman she devised a plan to shame the lad out of his waywardness.

It was New Year's Day, and Tom expected a present. His mother produced a small parcel. "It is nothing much, Tom," she said; "you know you were to have no New Year's gift unless your conduct improved greatly, and since Christmas I think you have been really worse than ever. Still I thought that perhaps this would be useful to you."

Tom tore off the paper eagerly, and found a small pocket diary. "Well," he said, after a pause, "it isn't much of a present, but I daresay it will come in handy." He thrust it carelessly into his already bulging pocket.

"Stay!" cried his mother, "give it back to me, please. I am going to keep that diary for you."

Tom stared.

"Now," said his mother, "I am going to make this diary a coloured record of your life. You see there is a space for each day's entry. In these spaces I shall paint in marks with my colours. Every day when you have been naughty, bad tempered, and self-willed all the day through, I shall paint in a black mark; on days when you have been naughty for the most part, but still trying to be good, I shall paint in a red mark; when you have been more good than naughty, I shall put in a blue mark; and on days when you have been bright and helpful and obedient all the day through, I shall fill the space in with gold. I am doing this because I want to make you think about the days of your youth. Go now, my boy, and try if you can't fill the year with golden days."

What Tom replied is best left unsaid.

He felt ashamed afterwards, and made a sort of resolve that the diary should be coloured throughout in blue and gold. But the resolve was soon forgotten.

On the last day of the year Tom's mother handed over the pocket-book to him. "Look it through carefully," she said, "then come with it to me."

Tom carried the book off to his own room, and turned page after page with eager haste. Soon his cheeks flushed, the flush deepened, and tears, real tears, stood in his eyes, and almost overflowed. Every page had its black day, some had two and three, very many days were marked red, a few only blue, and from beginning to end there was not one golden day! Tom knelt down, "O Lord!" he groaned, "I'm going to have another shot at it. Help me to get some golden days." Then he looked through the diary again. There were four days together left blank, what did that mean? Tom puzzled for a minute. Suddenly a gleam crossed his face. He ran down quickly, opened his mother's box,

dipped a brush in liquid gold, and filled
in each blank space with a shining dab.
Then he went to his mother.

"Well?" she said.

Tom placed the book silently in her
hands.

"My poor boy!" she exclaimed, "so
there was not one——" She stopped in
surprise. "Why, what is this, four days
marked with gold?"

Tom hung his head. "I did it, mother,"
he said. "I was so ashamed not to have
one golden day, and then I saw those
blank spaces, and I remembered I had
influenza then. You know how bad I was,
and in bed. I thought I couldn't have
been naughty those days, I was too ill, so
I got your box and marked them with
gold."

There was a long pause. Then Tom's
mother said, "So my dear lad was only
really good all last year on the four days
he was too ill to be naughty!"

"I'm going to try again, mother. I've
told the Lord so." Another long pause.

"But, mother, I did try last year, a little anyway. Why didn't I succeed?"

"Perhaps, Tom, because you didn't ask God to help you."

"But I said my prayers every day, mother."

Tom's mother smiled. "Ah! my lad, saying your prayers is one thing, praying is quite another."

"How, mother?"

"You said just now you told the Lord you were going to try again. What did you tell Him?"

"Why," said Tom, "I told Him I was going to have another shot at these golden days, and asked Him to help me."

Tom's mother smiled again. "It sounds rather slangy, Tom, but that was praying."

Tom did try again. His mother coloured another diary for him. At the end of the year there was not a week without its golden day. A third year he tried. In this year there was not a single black day. A few were marked with red, but the greater number were coloured in blue or gold.   After that a coloured diary was no longer needed.   All Tom's days were blue or gold.   His mother never called him "Wayward Tom" now.   When she spoke of him to others there was a glad, proud look in her eyes, and she said, "My noble lad."

My dear young friends, will *you* try, by God's help, to make the days of your youth all golden days?

Fox Cubs and Vine Blossoms.

"Take us the foxes, the little foxes, that spoil the
    vineyards ;
For our vineyards are in blossom."
                        ·—Song of Songs, ii. 15 (R.V.).

THIS is a snatch of a very old song,
sung thousands of years ago by
busy workers in the vineyards of
Palestine. Perhaps these two lines are a
sort of chorus or refrain. The writer of
the Song of Songs puts them into the
mouth of his peasant heroine, as a musical
response to her lover's spring-tide ode,
and this couplet, brief as it is, contains an
assurance that amidst all the splendour,
the unwelcome splendour of a palace, the

village maiden still remembers, and still
longs for, the familiar scenes of home.
She longs again to gather lily and crocus,
to recline beneath the spreading boughs
of cypress and cedar, to go through the
vineyards and hear once more the merry
voices of the vine-dressers, singing, as in
this strain she now pours forth, of vines
in blossom, giving promise of a rich vintage, and of little cubs destined soon to
become full-grown greedy foxes or jackals,
and unless taken early and destroyed,
likely to work mischief amongst the clus-
ters of ripe grapes.

Now I think, my young friends, that in
this fragment of very ancient poetry we
may find one or two useful lessons hinted
at. You will notice that two things are
mentioned, and each is an early stage of
growth. Little fox cubs, hardly big enough
or strong enough to carry off a day-old
chick, but sure to grow up some day, if
left alone, into destructive animals; and
blossoms, of little use as yet, but sure to
develop some day, if properly cared for,

into splendid bunches of grapes. But if
the grapes are to grow the cubs must stop
growing, or else when the grapes are ripe
the sly foxes grown ripe too in mischief
and cunning, will work sad havoc, and
the vines will be spoilt indeed. And so
the vine-dressers in their song remind
one another to be sure to catch the little
foxes, and never let them have a chance
of becoming big ones.

First, then, let this old song remind
you, both boys and girls, that your life
is in blossom, and that in due time your
manhood and womanhood should bear
fruit, courage, truth, righteousness, and
gentleness, patience, purity, and a great
deal beside. I don't mean that you
cannot have these virtues whilst you are
young. But they are only in the blossom
yet. Yet they have not grown into the
fully developed and ripe fruit. But the
blossom is beautiful, beautiful in itself,
and beautiful in the promise of something
still better to follow. Sometimes I see a
lad pouring over his school-books at night.

It is a summer evening. Through the open window come the voices of companions at play. He lifts his head, and for a moment gazes wistfully at the field across the road. He heard the thud of the ball against the bat, and the shout, "Well caught, Bob!" and he longs to rush out. Then he puts his fingers in his ears, leans his elbows upon the table, and busies himself in Euclid again. He will master that proposition, even if he gets no game at all to-night. "Well done, lad!" I say to myself. "That's beautiful blossom, if you go on like that the fruit will be splendid. Whatever you go in for, you will rise to the top."

Or it may be a girl I notice. She is absorbed in a most interesting story. In comes little sister, hot and rather cross, and shouts for mother. But mother is upstairs sleeping, for her rest was broken last night. Down goes the story-book; the hero was just about to deliver the heroine from a perilous position, but down goes the story-book, and for a whole hour little sister is told stories and shown pictures, and kept quiet that mother may sleep undisturbed. " Well done, dear girl ! " I say to myself. "This is beautiful blossom. Happy will be the man to whom some day the Lord grants the gathering of the grapes."

But alas ! sometimes it happens that the dear boys and girls whose youth was so full of blossom grow up into selfish or deceitful, or vain, or heartless men and women. The blossom was there, but when the ripe fruit should appear it is wanting. Why is this ? It is because some little cubs have grown into foxes and spoiled the vines. Dear young folk, you are fortunate indeed if you have had parents and friends who have been wise enough to look out for and take these little foxes before you were old enough to recognise and catch them yourselves. Perhaps in some cases you have not been thus blessed. Many a cub is allowed to live through the blindness or foolish indulgence of parents, and some of you

boys and girls may have a hard task
to take and destroy the half-grown foxes.

Three-year-old Tommy, not content
with his own Noah's ark, snatches Mary's
favourite doll. "Let him have it, little
darling," says mother; and so the mischievous cub selfishness thrives in the
vineyard, and Tommy will have a hard
tussle with it in later years.

Master Jack doesn't want to go to bed
when nurse comes for him. He clenches
his little fists and stamps in fury. "Oh!
doesn't he look funny!" cries father with
a burst of laughter; and the cub bad
temper is encouraged.

Susie, who is six years old, grumbles
unceasingly because the long-needed rain
is pouring precious drops upon the thirsty
earth, when Susie wanted to have a run
with her hoop. "Naughty rain!" says
Auntie, "it was too bad to spoil Susie's
afternoon;" and so the wretched little cub
peevishness is allowed to escape.

I need not multiply examples. You
will see how possible it is that before

boys and girls are ten years old, the little cubs may have grown into middling-sized foxes, and have done already much mischief. Now, my young friends, I do want to warn you very kindly and seriously against these small faults of character. You know, each one of you, what are the faults you most easily fall into. Strive against them with all your might. Strangle them whilst they are still only half-grown, or they will destroy those beautiful fruits of goodness your life should bring forth. My eye fell one day upon a scrap I thought well worth preserving. It showed that a little girl understood something about catching and killing these fox cubs. There was to be a party at the house that evening. The table was laid, and in the centre stood a great dish of oranges. The little girl peeped in to look at the arrangements and enjoy the glitter of glass and silver. How delicious those oranges appeared! She glanced round the room to make sure that no one saw her, then took an orange from the dish and hurried away. But she knew she had done wrong. There was a cub to kill, and she resolved then and there to kill it. So she went back again, and put the orange on the dish, and as she replaced it she exclaimed aloud, " Sold again, Satan ! "

I should like to add one word for those of you who are far on in your teens. There is a blossom in your vineyards which presently should ripen into that most precious vintage love and home, and all the wealth of happiness that love and home bring. My young friends, you who are already standing on the threshold of manhood and womanhood, let me beg of you in God's name to guard your vineyard with jealous care against those little foxes which, if suffered, will destroy ruthlessly the highest earthly blessings your life gives promise of. Beware of foolish jesting ; beware of toying with edged tools or playing with fire ; beware of innocent and natural but unruly longings ; beware of mistaking for the gold

F

of true admiration the poor gilt of
shallow flattery; beware of thinking the
divine flame of love kindled within you
when there may be nothing more than
a passing fancy excited by some physical
excellence, or intellectual affinity. The
time will come when the blossom of your
youth may develop into that fair fruit of
which the Song of Songs gives this most
exquisite description :—

> " For love is as strong as death,
>   Many waters cannot quench love,
>   Neither can the floods drown it,
>   If a man would give all the substance of his
>   house for love,
>   He would utterly be contemned."

But many young men and women have
allowed the blossom to perish and the
fruit could never form. Many others have
given away the blossom, and when the
fruit formed they could not bestow it as
they would. Let nothing, my young
friends, rob you of this most precious
product of your vineyards. May God
enable you to detect and destroy those

little foxes whose ravages have in so many thousands of instances ruined this particular vine.

Yes, my young friends, the vineyards are indeed in blossom. As I look round on your bright happy faces, I see abundant promise of a rich vintage. I see the promise of many a true man and noble woman. Guard earnestly against those little faults which would prevent you from growing into such. There is an old proverb which runs, " Take care of the pence, and the pounds will take care of themselves." So I would say, " Suffer the little faults, and the big sins will look after themselves; but destroy the little faults, and the great faults will never have a chance." So next time, children, you are peevish, or envious, or jealous, or bad-tempered, or tempted to deceive, say, " Here comes another little cub, but by God's grace I will take it and slay it."

Work for Little Hands.

"Gather out the stones."—ISA. lxii. 10.

THE Prophet is speaking in this passage about a great highway that was to be made through the desert, along which God's people should pass in safety to their far-away and long lost but never forgotten country. It was a tremendous journey that was to be undertaken, but it was to be made easy for the people. Kind hearts and willing hands would construct a road right through the wilderness, that the "ransomed of the Lord might return, and come to Zion with songs and everlasting joy upon their heads."

Now if you have ever watched a gang of navvies constructing a road, you could not help but notice that the work was rough and hard. It was no child's play. Whether the road were of macadam, or sets, or wood blocks, or asphalt, or, like the roads the Romans made through this country hundreds of years ago, of solid flagstones, it needed the sturdy muscle of strong fullgrown men. The first part of this text is not for you young people : " Go through, go through the gates ; prepare ye the way of the people ; cast up, cast up the highway." That is work for leaders and men. But next comes a very simple duty, a piece of work that little hands can do, "Gather out the stones." For a perfect road must not only be solid and well laid, but it must also be clear of loose stones. A friend of mine was driving the other day along a fine broad high road when his horse stepped upon a loose stone and fell, and was so seriously injured that it had to be shot. What a difference it would have made if some boy or girl had gathered that stone and thrown it over the hedge! This then is what I call work for little hands, gathering out the stones.

Now if I were to ask you the question, What is the most important of all roads? I am sure some of you would answer, and answer rightly, The road to heaven. It is a road that has cost God a great deal to make for us, and that costs us a great deal to keep open. It needs constant repairing and constant guarding, because there are enemies always trying to destroy the road or to block it up. And there have been times in the history of this country when that road has been all but destroyed, and would have been quite, but great and strong men came to the front and cast up again the highway. It was almost completely blocked once by superstition; but Wycliffe, and Tyndale, and Coverdale, and Rogers, and Cranmer, and other great road-makers, forced a way through. In later ages it was almost destroyed by the widespread wickedness of the people; and Wesley and Whitfield,

and other road-makers with them, opened
it out again.   And to-day, hundreds of men
and women are working splendidly as God's
engineers and patrols, to preserve and
strengthen, or to defend this great highway
of souls.   And some day perhaps you will
grow strong enough and wise enough to
help in this great work ; but in the mean-
time, if you are good enough, though you
are only boys and girls, you may render
useful service by gathering out the stones.

By gathering out the stones, I mean
removing those little difficulties and hind-
rances which lie in the path, and so making
the road to heaven easier for people to
tread.   For example, mother comes in,
tired and hot.   She has been baking and
attending to the house all morning, and
out shopping this afternoon, and there will
be mending and darning to-night.   And
just as she comes in baby wakes up and
begins to cry, and mother exclaims wearily,
"Oh dear me, why did you wake up just
now, baby?"   Then up speaks little ten-
year-old Susie, who has just come in from

school, "You go and rest a little bit,
mother dear, and I'll play with baby and
keep him good." And so Susie gathered a
stone out of the way, and made mother's
path easier for her.

Katie was rather cross because she
could not get a sum right; she hated
home lessons, she said, and tears filled her
eyes. "Oh, you little cry-baby," said
Harold, and by saying that he just put
another stone in his sister's way. But Jack
threw down the tale he was reading, and
said, "Let me see if I can't find out where
you've gone wrong?" And soon the light
was dancing in Katie's eyes again, for Jack
had gathered a stone out of the path.

An old woman was creeping slowly up
the steep street carrying a heavy basket.
She was very poor, and her lot was a hard
one, and she was thinking to herself, "If
I'd been grandly dressed they'd have sent
it home for me, if it had only been a pound
of sugar. But no one cares for the likes of
me." And she began to wonder whether
God was really kind. But just then Tom

came running down the street. His uncle
had given him sixpence, and he was hurry-
ing off to buy a ball. But he noticed how
weary and worn the poor old dame looked.
He knew her at once. It was widow
Johnson, whose husband had been killed
on the line. He crossed over, and said,
"Let me carry this for you." And when
he had put the basket on the bare table
in the bare little room, he said, "You
haven't very much furniture." He thought
of his ball, and almost wished he hadn't
met the widow toiling up the hill. Then
he glanced round the room again, and
pulling out his sixpence, said shyly,
"Perhaps that would buy you a bit more,"
and ran off. But a tear came into the old
woman's eye, and as she wiped it away
with her apron, she said, "The dear Lord
hasn't forgotten me after all." Tom had
gathered a stone out of the way, and made
her path to heaven easier.

You will be able to think of many more
examples for yourselves, but these few will
make clear to you what I mean by gather-

ing out the stones. But do not make the
mistake of some young people, who dream
grand dreams of grand things they will do
when they are men and women to improve
the road to heaven, but cannot see the
stones close to them which they might
gather out of the way.

Jenny lay back in the arm-chair one
wintry afternoon. Her feet were on the
fender, and the glow of the fire lighted up
her face.   There was a happy dreamy
expression upon it. Outside it was bleak
and cold, but Jenny was wrapped in comfort and profound thought.   Andersen's
Fairy Tales lay in her lap, and she was
thinking how much good she would do if
she were a fairy. There should not be a
poor woman in the country, nor a starving
child, nor a man out of work; and
wherever she went she would make people
happy. Oh! she would do so much good,
and make the way to heaven so easy.
Just then the door opened, and Jenny's
mother said, " Here, my little girl, just put
on your things and take this jug of soup to

poor old William." Jenny gave a great start, and then exclaimed, in the worst humour, "Oh! bother the soup. Won't it do to-morrow? I was having such a nice time."

Poor Jenny! She was dreaming of what she would do if she were only chief engineer on the Lord's highway, but she was not willing simply to gather out the stones. She would have waved her magic wand to benefit thousands, but she was not ready to go into the next street to cheer a feeble old man with a quart of soup!

Dear young folk, don't make that mistake; but daily, by helpful words and by acts of thoughtful kindness, try to make their path easier to those about you, and Jesus Christ, the great Master of the highway, will surely reward you, who, in thus gathering out the stones, become little road-menders for Him.

A Bad Burial.

" Buried with the burial of an ass."—JER. xxii. 19.

I AM afraid we do not think very much about living donkeys. They are often hard worked and badly treated, and generally spoken of as "stupid." Though I would have you remember, my young friends, that in the case of one famous animal that figures on a page of Scripture, the master mistook his own stupidity for his donkey's; and if you observe closely men and animals, you will find that this is just the case with many modern masters and donkeys. But who cares anything at all about a dead donkey? and what sort of a funeral would it get?

Would anybody dig a grave for the deceased ass, and put up a neat headstone to mark its resting-place? The prophet Jeremiah tells us what they did with dead donkeys at Jerusalem in his day. They dragged the poor beast out of the city, and threw it on one of the great rubbish mounds in the valley outside the walls where the city's refuse was deposited. And there the jackals would gather, and the vultures swoop down, and tear the flesh off the carcase until but the clean dry bones were left bleaching in the hot sunshine. That was the burial of an ass. Now the prophet, speaking of a certain person, says he should have just such a funeral as that. Think what a dreadful thing! No one to mourn for him; no one to dig a grave for him, no one to be able afterwards to find the spot where his body had been laid to rest! This man was to be rudely dragged through the streets, and thrown on a rubbish heap, and his body left for beasts and birds of prey to devour. Surely you will think it must have been some wretched pauper whom nobody owned or cared for, and so the sanitary authorities got rid of his body in the quickest and cheapest way possible. But no, it was the corpse of a great man that was to be thus disposed of,—of no less a man than a king! It was, in fact, of Jehoiakim, king of Judah, of whom Jeremiah the prophet foretold he should be "buried with the burial of an ass." Whilst he lived, it was "Long live the king!" and "May it please your Majesty," and so forth. But he was so hated and despised for his misdeeds, that when his enemies had killed him, there should not a man be found who would take the trouble to scratch a hole in the ground to put him into, and he would be cast forth therefore like a dead donkey!

I want this to teach you, my young friends, that when people die they are valued at their proper worth. In these enlightened days the State would not permit any body, even a donkey's, to be cast out and left to rot near a great town.

The very worst villain is sure of some sort
of a funeral. And yet there are many
men of whom it may be said that they
are "buried with the burial of an ass."
Sometimes there will be a grand funeral.
The hearse will be covered with plumes,
and drawn by magnificent horses ; the coffin
will be of polished oak, with silver mount-
ings. A great many mourning coaches
will follow. The vault will be a costly
one, and over it will be placed a splendid
monolith, adorned with little figures and
big lies cut in the solid stone. But with
all this costly array there will not be one
single tear. The mourners, as they call
them, all wear black clothes, and find it
hard not to look cheerful as they ride to
the cemetery. And afterwards people say,
What a happy release it is, not for the
man who has been interred, but for his
widow and children ! That is being "buried
with the burial of an ass."

In a graveyard I used to know well, they
told me there had once been a stone which
bore this inscription :—

> " Here lies a man who did no good,
> And if he'd lived he never would ;
> And where he's gone, and how he fares,
> Nobody knows, and nobody cares."

That man was "buried with the burial of an ass."

I have been at many sad funerals, where there were broken hearts, and eyes red with prolonged weeping ; but the saddest funerals of all I have attended, have been one or two dry-eyed burials, where every one tried to look melancholy, but secretly rejoiced that a useless and mischievous life had been cut short. Remember, dear young people, you who have so many golden opportunities coming to you every day, if you neglect those opportunities, if you do not become good and kind, and true and helpful, however rich or powerful you might become, that is the sort of funeral you will have, you will be " buried with the burial of an ass."

But, on the other hand, if you have lived a pure and beautiful life, however poor or unknown you may be, it will have a happy ending; and even though a mere handful of people should follow you to the grave, those few will shed tears for you that will be a more precious memorial than the costliest mausoleum. I think just now of a dear good man I once knew. He was very poor, miserably poor, earning only just enough by odd jobs as a cobbler to keep body and soul together. But his character was beautifully Christ-like, and when he died what a funeral he had! Rich and poor gathered round his grave, and lamented together that one of the best men in the village, perhaps the best, had been removed from their midst.

It is a sad fact that every day men—ay, and women too—are being " buried with the burial of an ass." May God help you so to live, walking in the footsteps of Jesus Christ, that when your time comes it shall be very different. May there be many to weep for you, and to offer at your grave this prayer, " Grant, Lord, that we may meet our loved one again."

G

Love, the Philoso= pher's Stone.

"So the last shall be first."—MATT. xx. 16.

THREE centuries ago the scientific men of Europe were bent on discovering a wonderful and precious substance known as the philosopher's stone. It was the peculiar property of this undiscovered substance that any common metal it came into contact with would be transformed by its magic charm into pure gold. And you will easily understand therefore, that in an age when the belief in such a substance was very strong, the search after it would be very keen. That search has long since

ended; we no longer believe that there
is any such marvellous substance. But
I am going to speak to you of something
which is like the imagined philosopher's
stone in this respect, that it transforms
very common things, common thoughts,
common words, common deeds, and gives
to them in God's sight a new and in-
finitely greater value. This is the lesson
taught us by the Lord Jesus Christ in the
parable of the labourers in the vineyard.

These first sixteen verses in the twentieth
chapter of St Matthew's Gospel have greatly
puzzled many people. Some have said
they seem to teach that if a man has
lived an idle life all his days, but repents
just at the last, he will be as well off in
the next world as if he had been working
hard for God from his childhood. Others
say they are sure Jesus Christ cannot
mean that, but what He does mean
they cannot make out. Now I believe
a great deal of this difficulty arises from
the habit many people have of reading
their Bible in chapters. If you begin

where this parable begins, at the twentieth chapter of St Matthew's Gospel, and do not take particular notice of what is recorded in the nineteenth chapter as leading up to the parable, you are certain to be puzzled by it. Something had led Jesus Christ to say that many who stand at the bottom in this life will come to the top in the kingdom of God, and many that are at the top now will go down to the bottom. Read carefully the last verse of the nineteenth chapter, " But many that are first shall be last ; and the last shall be first." And then to explain that, He goes on, " FOR the kingdom of heaven is like unto a man that is an householder, which went out early in the morning to hire labourers into his vineyard." And then having finished his story, Jesus Christ ends it as he began it, " So the last shall be first, and the first last."

Now let us turn back, and see what led our Lord in the first instance to make this strange statement. There is the rich young ruler disappearing in the distance,

He has gone away sad and disappointed. He wanted salvation, and he was prepared to pay a big price for it, but when, in answer to his question as to how much it would cost him, Jesus Christ in the calmest way asked for *everything*, he went away pained. But Peter was feeling particularly happy at the moment. " Behold," he said, " WE (with great emphasis on the "we") *have* forsaken ALL, and followed Thee." Then turning over in his own mind Jesus Christ's promise to the young ruler, that if he gave up everything he should have treasure in heaven, Peter inquired, with a keen eye to his own interests and his companions', " What shall WE have therefore ? " True, Peter's all did not amount to much—a cottage, a share in a fishing-boat, and some fisherman's tackle. The wealthy ruler could have bought up the whole lot and never have felt it. Still it was Peter's all. He had truly made a complete sacrifice, and he evidently considered that that full surrender of everything would entitle him to the highest rewards to be bestowed. Our Lord's reply put matters in a new light for Peter. Every one, He said, who sacrificed in any way present interests for His name's sake, should have an ample reward here and hereafter. BUT— But what? Well, the rewards would not be given necessarily on the method Peter was thinking of—the big rewards to those who had sacrificed most, and the smallest to those who had sacrificed least. "But many that are first (at the top of the subscription list) shall be last (in the amount of reward bestowed), and the last (like the widow who cast in two mites, Luke xxi. 1-4) shall be first" (in Christ's notice and praise). And then, to explain *why* this would be so, our Lord added the parable of the labourers in the vineyard.

And now, my young friends, glance for a moment at this parable, and then I think you will see what I meant by saying that there is a something which gives to our smallest, poorest offerings a wonderful value, and, like the philosopher's stone,

transforms our gifts of base metal into
gifts of gold. You will notice that there
are two classes of labourers in this parable,
namely, those who put money before work,
and those who put work before money.
The men who go into the vineyard first,
and who work through a twelve hours'
day, "agree" for a penny—that is, for a
denarius, a silver coin worth about eight-
pence-halfpenny of our money—as their
day's wage. You must take special notice
of that word "*agree*," for the significance
of the parable turns upon it. They struck
a bargain. They are not blamed for doing
so, but the point to be marked is this,
they put their own interest first. Their
first thought was, How much money can
we get? their after-thought, How much
work can we do? The other men made
no bargain. They left the matter of wage
to the master. Their first thought was,
He will give us work. Their after-thought,
We shall get what we deserve. When the
day was over the men were called together
to receive their wage, and beginning with

the last-comers the steward gave "each man a penny." They had only worked an hour. They had *earned* therefore one-twelfth of a penny. The rest was not wage, but *reward*. Reward for what? For the spirit in which they had worked, for their trustfulness, for their gratitude, for their desire to please. Perhaps also it was partly *compensation*—compensation for those long hours of anxious weary waiting during which they had seen their fellows engaged and no man had hired them. Now when the men who had been working from six in the morning saw these men who only started work at five o'clock in the afternoon, receiving each one a penny, precisely the same thought that was in Peter's mind, and which he uttered, occurred to them, "What shall WE have therefore?" "And they likewise received every man a penny." That is, they got exactly what they bargained for, and no more. And so Jesus Christ gave Peter to understand, that he must not think because he had forsaken all to follow Him, he would therefore receive the highest reward. *Why* had he forsaken all? Was it altogether for Christ's sake, or was it largely for his own? What was the motive underlying his service? Because that would greatly determine the amount of his recompense. Reward he should surely have, but not necessarily the highest; because the smallest services inspired by pure devotion to God would be valued more highly, and rewarded more amply, than the highest sacrifices prompted by self-interest.

Now, my dear young friends, what is at the bottom of *your* religion? Are you denying yourselves, and trying to obey God, because you want to escape hell, or because you long to enter heaven? Then you will have your reward, but not the highest reward. Is your feeling, "He loved me, and gave Himself for me," therefore I delight to do all I can for Him? Then indeed your smallest gifts, your smallest services, will be precious in God's sight.

I knew a gentleman who once put a half-sovereign in the collection-box in mistake for a sixpence. He was ashamed to ask for it back, for he was well-to-do; but he comforted himself by saying, "Ah, well, I reckon I shall get credit for it up there." But if I have made the teaching of this parable clear to you, you will be sure that "up there" that piece of gold would be entered as a sixpence.

A little girl had a penny in her pocket. It had been given to her that Sunday morning, and she was longing for Monday to come that she might spend it. But during the morning service the preacher pleaded the cause of hospitals, and spoke of the sad cases of suffering relieved in them. The little girl listened with all her ears. Then she said softly, "O God, I do love You, and I'm going to give You my penny for those sick people of Yours," and she dropped her coin into the box. But in God's eyes that penny shone with a gleam of gold, for it had been touched by LOVE, the Philosopher's Stone!

The Sacred Cup.

"And He took the cup."—MATT. xxvi. 27.

IF any of you had in your own house the very vessel that Jesus Christ handed round to His disciples at this sad farewell supper, I am sure you would count it your greatest treasure. It would be a relic of priceless worth. Men would travel thousands of miles to see it, and would gaze upon it with reverent awe. Now, what *did* become of that cup? Was it kept and prized, and if so, by whom? Was it handed down from generation to generation, and if so, for how long was it preserved? These are interesting questions, but there is no answer to them. The probability is that the clothes Jesus Christ wore, the furniture He used, the cross upon which He died, all perished very quickly, and that in a little time not one keepsake remained.   But if we know nothing as to what became of this cup from actual history, tradition has gathered around it some wonderful stories.   I must warn you that these stories are purely fanciful, and some of them are extravagant, even stupid. But some of them are beautiful, and although not true in themselves, the truth shines exquisitely through them.   Taken together, these curious fancies constitute what is known as the legend of the Holy Grail.

The story runs that this *Grail*, or cup, came into the possession of Joseph of Arimathea, and that when in later years Joseph came over to England to preach the Gospel to our savage forefathers he brought the holy cup with him.   It was an object of most remarkable beauty, and possessed some extraordinary properties. Its colour was a rich transparent ruby-red ;

a halo of glory shone round about it, and dazzling rays streamed from it; and whoever possessed this cup was secure against every ill. It supplied miraculously every kind of want, and simply to gaze upon it was to be healed of any disease. And so for many years, during which England was passing out of heathenism into Christian civilisation, the Holy Grail was the glory of the land. But in later years there was a relapse into heathenism, and then this sacred cup was taken up into heaven away from the sight of wicked men, and only very rarely indeed was a glimpse of it seen, and then only by people of perfectly stainless life.

Now you are all familiar of course with the name of the good King Arthur, that best and bravest of kings. One of the knights of his Round Table was Sir Percival. This Sir Percival had a sister, who was a nun, and she, having been filled with heavenly joy by a vision of the Holy Grail, described it to Sir Percival; and Sir Percival described it to the knights of the

Round Table; and the knights, fired with holy enthusiasm, took an oath that they would ride a whole twelvemonth in quest of this glorious object. When they returned at the year's end, King Arthur asked them if they had seen the Holy Grail. Only Sir Galahad, Sir Bors, and Sir Percival had seen the sacred cup. They were the three truest, and bravest, and purest of all the knights. Sir Lancelot had been bitterly disappointed; the vision indeed appeared to him, but a covering of crimson samite thrown over the cup hid it from his sight.

> "What I saw was veiled
> And covered; and this quest was not for me."

And the cause of this disappointment was a secret sin long cherished by the knight. Because of the stain upon his soul, he could not see the Grail itself; but because of his deep remorse, and his desire to prevail against temptation, he was permitted to see the veiled outline of the glorious object.

Now, can you, my young friends, puzzle out any meaning in this curious old legend? Is there any vision of glory for men to-day, a vision which only the true and pure hearted can behold, but which once beheld makes the poor rich, and the wretched happy, and the sick whole? Perhaps you think, Certainly not. Yet the Lord Jesus Christ speaks of such a vision, and that too in a little verse which is very familiar to you. You have heard it many a time. "Blessed are the pure in heart, for they shall see God." Do not suppose that means the pure in heart shall gain heaven at last, and see God there. Our Saviour means, that in this life those who are truly pure in heart will live in the perpetual consciousness of God's loving presence. Not with the bodily eye, but with the soul's eye they see God, and this glad vision cures for them all the ills of life. There is a certain verse of a hymn—I daresay you know it well—of which I have heard people make great fun,—

"With Thee conversing, we forget
　All time, and toil, and care ;
Labour is rest, and pain is sweet,
　If Thou my God art here."

They say the man who penned those lines
can never have had a bad toothache.
That is but shallow criticism. The writer
does not say that pain in itself is sweet; but
he says, that if pain brings us into a joyous
sense of God's nearness to us, then there is
a sweetness in it. And, my dear young
friends, just what the Holy Grail was
supposed to do in olden days in bringing
peace and comfort and blessing to the
troubled and needy, this vision of God does
for men and women,—yes, and for boys
and girls, to-day. I am thinking just now
of some of the happiest people I have ever
known. There was the dear old blind lady
living in a little cottage in a Berkshire
village, with only just enough to keep body
and soul together ; her heart was full of
sunshine, and she went from house to
house, wherever there was sickness or
sorrow, to carry there the secret of her

own happiness. There was the Yorkshire clog-maker, working still at his trade in his eighty-fourth year to keep himself and his old wife out of the workhouse, his face always lighted up with a smile, and his heart overflowing with thankfulness, and his speech as one who held converse with angels. There was. the bed-ridden old widow in a little Lancashire town living in a cottage that disgraced this nineteenth-century civilisation; her talk was all of God's goodness, and of the love that was making ready for her a mansion in the skies. These were amongst the happiest people I have ever known. They were pure in heart, and they saw God.

Dear young people, you naturally long for health, and success, and pleasure, and you think these things will make you happy. But this is the secret of deep and lasting joy, — pray to have pure hearts. Then you will have this vision of God, and it will bring with it a gladness that nothing can rob you of.

And now, to stamp upon your minds the

teaching of this legend of the Holy Grail,
I will commit it to verse for you, and
perhaps sometime you will commit the
verses to memory.

THE LEGEND OF THE HOLY GRAIL.

O Mystic Cup! of roseate hue,
By many sought, beheld by few,
And they the truest of the true!
Though shrined in myth, we would not fail
To grasp the truth beneath the veil,
And know thy meaning, Holy Grail.

As in that holiest place of all,
Through rifts in curtain and in wall
The year-old dust lay like a pall,—
Lay thick on Cherubs' outstretched wings,
Lay thick on ark, and staves, and rings,
And hid the Temple's precious things;—

And there, beneath Time's slow-laid sheet,
Touched by the Cherubs' wingèd feet,
Lo! the pure golden Mercy-seat!
So would we search, with quickened eyes,
And find beneath strange vanities
Some treasured thought to keep and prize.

Surely, O Sacred Cup, thou art
Some joy from sinful life apart,
Some secret of a stainless heart;
Surely the knights who ride in quest
Are they who follow Truth's behest,
And boldly leave with God the rest.

O fairest joy, of Heavenly birth!
O joy beyond all joys of earth,
Beyond all wealth, and pomp, and mirth!
The pure in heart, who seek aright,
Shall gaze upon the vision bright
That turns all darkness into light,—

That turns all present loss to gain,
That turns to good all present pain,
And yields a cure for every bane!
In this sweet meaning of the tale,
Long may the Holy Quest prevail,
And eager eyes behold the Grail!

The Secret of a Fall.

"But Peter followed Him afar off."—MATT. xxvi. 58.

TWO or three years ago a very beautiful star shone night after night for several weeks with unusual lustre and brilliancy. Everybody was talking about it, and many people thought it must be some new celestial body, or perhaps some star long lost to sight that had reappeared. And some people wondered if it was the star of Bethlehem shining again in these days of ours! Now, as a matter of fact, it was no new star at all, but a very old friend, that everybody had seen before, over and over again. It was the planet Venus, but it was shining with uncommon brightness because it had reached its nearest approach to the sun. It had come closer to our great luminary by some thousands of miles than it had been for many a year, or would be for many a year again, and so it shone out with more than its wonted glory. But Uranus and Neptune, two sister planets, are so far away that they have not any ordinary brightness, and must be viewed through a telescope to be seen at all.

If I were to ask you, Are there any other heavenly bodies shining in the light of our sun? you would answer at once, " Yes, comets." But you young people have never seen a comet, unless you have had a golden opportunity some time of sweeping the skies with a powerful telescope, when a comet was within range of telescopic vision. How is it that we do not see comets in the sky every night? Because they are far far away, beyond the orbit of the outermost planets, and we can only see them when they come from infinite space and pursue their path for a little while in the neighbourhood of the

sun.   Then, as they recede, they grow
dimmer and dimmer, until they are lost
again in infinite distance.

And, once again, if I were to ask you,
Are any of the heavenly bodies ever blotted
out so that for awhile we cannot see them ?
you would answer, "Oh yes, you mean
eclipses." That is what I do mean. Sometimes the moon hides a planet from us,
and sometimes a fixed star, and sometimes
even the sun itself.

Now I want to remind you that the
prophet Malachi foretold in a beautiful
passage that the Sun of Righteousness
should arise with healing in His wings ; and
that St Luke, speaking of the birth of Jesus
Christ, said that the sunrising had dawned
upon the people. Whilst Jesus Christ,
then, is the Sun of Righteousness, shining
with infinite brightness by the splendour
of His own goodness, His disciples, like
the planets, derive the brightness of their
lives from Him. And sometimes men
come to Jesus Christ, and for a little while
shine in His light, and then, like the comets,

fly off, and their brightness fades away! And sometimes the light of true disciples goes out, because something comes between them and their Lord, and there is an eclipse. It was so with Peter, even though Jesus Christ warned him beforehand. "Simon, Simon," He said, "Satan has asked, and obtained leave to put all of you through his sieve, as men separate chaff from grain; but, Peter, I have prayed for thee that thy faith may not be eclipsed" (Luke xxii. 31, 32). *Eclipsed* was the very word used, as you may see for yourselves when you begin to read your New Testament in Greek. And how soon it came true! Only a few hours later, Peter was cursing and swearing, and declaring that he had never had anything to do with Jesus Christ, and did not even know Him. And in that hour all the light and beauty of Peter's character was completely blotted out, there was a total eclipse of his faith!

Now if you have read carefully this sad story of Peter's fall, and that fine passage a little before which describes how Peter

alone of all the disciples had the faith and
courage to say right out that he believed
Jesus to be the Son of God, it must seem
to you a wonderful thing that such a man
could fall into such a sin.   How could
Peter do such a thing?   I remember once
reading the narrative, and these thoughts
were in my mind.   Then I went carefully
back, step by step, to see if I could trace
the point where Peter first went distinctly
astray, and thus presently I came to this
morning's text, " But Peter followed afar
off."   Then at once I saw that I had
lighted upon the secret of Peter's fall.
" Afar off ! "   He was still a disciple, but a
distant one, and the farther he got from
Christ, the dimmer became the light of
truth in him.   " Afar off," until at last a
servant girl came between Christ and
Peter, to whom he dare not own that he
even knew his Lord !   Think how different
it would have been, if, when the soldiers
led Christ away, Peter had boldly gone to
Him, and passed his arm through his
Master's, and said firmly, " Lord, I will

walk with Thee." Then, instead of suffering eclipse, he would have shone as a star
of the first magnitude! But when he
slunk back, and followed afar off, he prepared the way for the terrible fall that
followed.

Dear young people, if you would shine,
keep near to Jesus Christ, and don't be
ashamed to confess Him. It was easy
and delightful for Peter to keep near Christ
when He was healing the people, and
feeding the multitude, and when His praises
were in all mouths. But it was quite
another thing, when Jesus was surrounded
only by soldiers and bitter enemies. And
it is easy for you to keep near Jesus when
you are amongst good people who love
His name. But if you would be bright
Christians, keep near Jesus when you are
amongst those who do not love Him or
honour Him. Don't be afraid of saying,
" I belong to Jesus. I can't do what you
want me to, or go where you invite me."
Don't slink behind at such times, as if
Christ were nothing to you. If you do,

you will soon be following far off; and next will come some sad fall, for which you will have bitterly to grieve.

But perhaps you wonder how you are to get near to Jesus. Read carefully, again and again, the record in the Gospels of what He said and did, and how He lived. Pray earnestly that your life may be like His, in kindness, and truth, and purity; and He Himself, in a way I cannot explain to you, but which you will find out, will bring you close to Him, and your life will shine with the brilliant lustre of the evening star at its nearest approach to the sun.

Pleasure and Duty : A Parable.

"Whosoever will save his life shall lose it ; but whosoever will lose his life for My sake, the same shall save it."—LUKE ix. 24.

AN old man called his son to him. "My son," said he, "thou hast tarried with me many years, now thou must go forth upon thy journey. Take heed to thy steps, and remember these my words,— the easiest way is oft-times the hardest, the shortest road the longest, and the kindest stranger thy worst enemy."

So the young man journeyed forth, and his father's words sounded strange in his ears. "What can they mean?" thought he. " I know not what they mean ; " and straightway he forgot them. Outside the city gates there met him a fair damsel. Her face was pleasant to look upon, and her voice sweet to the ears. On her head she wore a wreath of ivy and vine leaves intertwined. " Come with me," she said, " my name is Pleasure. I wander through grassy meadows, and linger by sparkling brooks. My home is a palace. I am the sworn foe of Care and Sorrow. Come with me. Before thee, on the road thou art treading, are hardship and peril. Come with me, and thou shalt save thy life."

Now, on the other side of the road stood an old man. His face was marked with deep furrows, and its expression grave, even stern, and he stooped as if under the weight of years. " My son," said he, " come thou with me. I will show thee the path of life through the valley of the shadow of death. I will lead thee to fulness of joy and to pleasures for evermore."

" What is thy name, old man ?" said the

youth. "My name is Duty," he replied. "Care and Sorrow are my sisters. By strange paths they have led many into life, but Pleasure with her vain deceits hath fooled more to their destruction. Come thou with me, my son."

"Nay," cried the youth, "thy face is forbidding, Duty, and I fear the ways of thy sisters Care and Sorrow. I will go with Pleasure." So they turned aside down a shady lane. The deadly night-shade, and poppy, and hemlock, and fox-glove grew thickly in the hedges. Over-head the trees were laden with fruits. They were ripe and luscious to the eye, and the youth took them freely at Pleasure's bidding, but always to experience a horrible nausea following. They passed over grassy fields. From afar they looked lovely in their greenness, but the grass was thin, and the field strewn with sharp flints. And the sparkling brooks sparkled only when a chance sunbeam, breaking through heavy clouds, touched their muddy waters. Presently they reached a beautiful palace.

"Now," said Pleasure, "let thy soul dwell at ease." In the splendid banqueting hall the table groaned beneath a variety of dishes. The youth, faint with hunger, sat down to eat. Another fair damsel waited. Her eyes were full of laughter, and her lips scornful, and her name was Disappointment. The viands were rich and highly seasoned, but the more the youth ate the more he hungered ; the wines were choice and rare, but the more he drank the more he thirsted. When the meal was over he looked for Pleasure, but she had disappeared. "We are her sisters," said Disappointment, "Despair and I, and we wait upon those whom Pleasure brings here." "And where," asked the youth, "is Despair ? " "She will appear presently," she replied, and the laughter leaped in her eyes. Now the night grew chilly, and the youth drew near the great fireplace. Disappointment piled on the logs, till the fierce flame scorched him, yet the hotter the flame became the more he shivered with cold. "Come," said Disappointment, "I

will lead thee to thy chamber." The room
was luxurious in its furnishing. The bed
was soft and downy, but it yielded no
warmth; drowsiness crept over the youth,
but he slept not, for his father's words
haunted him, "Take heed." So he lay
with closed eyes and open ears. Now the
windows of the chamber opened upon a
balcony, and beneath the balcony flowed a
black, deep, swift stream, and the name of
that stream is Destruction. In a little
while Disappointment entered the chamber
softly, and with her came her sister Despair.
They stood and looked upon the youth,
and he heard Despair whisper, " Poor fool !
nearly asleep, and then we will cast him
into the stream." So they withdrew awhile.
Then indeed the youth roused himself,
and sought to escape. In vain ! the door
was locked. But spying round carefully,
presently he noticed a key hanging high
upon the wall over against the door, and
beneath the key these words :—

" This key Repentance is ; take thou this key ;
   Death waits thee here, be wise and flee."

So he stretched forth his hand to take it. But the key hung high. Once, twice, thrice he tried in vain. At last by a desperate leap he grasped it, opened the door, and fled.

Now retracing his steps the youth found Duty still standing by the highway. "Art thou escaped, my son?" said he; "come then with me."

"But thy face is stern," said the youth, "and thy voice harsh, and I am afraid of thee."

"My son," said the old man, "Duty seems ever thus to those who know him not. But fear naught. Come thou with me." So they journeyed together. The night was dark, but Duty carried a lamp by a chain, and the light swung near the ground, making a bright circle for their feet. Yet when the wind blew hard, the youth feared the lamp would be put out. "Fear not, my son," said Duty, "this lamp is truth, and its light never dies."

The path grew steep and rough, and the youth was ready to sink down through fatigue. So he wept and cried, "Let us turn back, Duty, for my strength fails me." But the old man said, "Nay, my son. Weeping may endure for a night, but joy cometh in the morning. And thy strength is small, because thou hast abode awhile in Pleasure's palace. Few escape with their life, and none who have feasted at Pleasure's table escape without loss of strength. But courage, my son, thou shalt prevail yet."

Now, when the morning broke, behold at the youth's side a radiant angel whose face shone with a smile of heavenly beauty. "Who art thou?" said the youth. "I am Duty," said he, "who led thee along the steep track through the dark night." "Duty?" cried the youth, "how thou art changed!"

"Nay, my son," said Duty, "but thy vision was dim before, and Pleasure had bewitched thine eyes."

Henceforth the road became easy, flowers sprung up at every step, the sun shone out strongly and light breezes tempered the

I

heat, and fruit trees heavily laden grew in the highway. But the youth feared to eat. "Thou mayest take freely," said Duty, "with me at thy side. Let thy soul delight itself in fatness, for thou hast entered into life."

The Lord's Surprise Visits.

"In an hour that ye think not."—LUKE xii. 40 (R.V.).

THERE is a certain official of whom teachers and scholars alike, in Public Elementary Schools, stand in some awe, I mean Her Majesty's Inspector; and there is one particular kind of attention he gives to schools which especially tends towards regular discipline and good order. The period of annual inspection is indeed a critical time, not to be looked forward to without sundry misgivings. But that at least is a sure thing. The thing that is altogether uncertain, and that calls for constant watchfulness, is the surprise visit. If all is in proper working order, it is a matter of no moment; it is even something to be thankful for. But how awkward, if any disorder happens to prevail, or the expected conditions of school life are in any way unfulfilled, and unless from day to day everything is done as the Code requires it may easily be so, for the Inspector is almost sure to come at an hour when you think not.

Now this text speaks of the Lord making "surprise visits" to His people. And it tells further of the dismay and alarm of those servants who at their Lord's sudden appearance are found wasting their time and neglecting their duty. I do not want to frighten you, my young friends, but just think how many men have been called suddenly into their Lord's presence in the very midst of their forgetfulness and disobedience. And think how you yourself would feel if just when you were in some place where you ought not to be, or with some company you ought not to be with, or doing something or saying something you ought not to do or to say, a voice should suddenly cry in your ears, " Thy soul is required of thee." It might easily be so, and you are only safe by being always in your right place, and doing always your proper duty. But if this text speaks of some servants to whom their Lord's surprise visit was a painful thing, it speaks of others also to whom it was a great joy. And when He suddenly came, " happy were they." And I want to speak to you of these happy surprises, and to point out to you that at times and in ways altogether unexpected the Lord really does present Himself before His people. And in order to make this plain, I am going to tell you a very old story. I do not profess that it is entirely a true story. But just as a nut without itself being eatable contains a kernel, which with a little trouble you may get at and find very good, so this story, without being true, contains a truth and a very blessed one, at which we may arrive by a little thought, and from which we may derive both comfort and help.

Once upon a time, then, about one hundred years after Jesus Christ left this earth, there lived in Jesus Christ's country a man of enormous strength and gigantic stature. His name was Offero, and he wanted to find a master. But because he was a proud man, he scorned the idea of obeying any master weaker than himself. At length he heard of a certain king before whose might the whole world trembled, and into that monarch's service the giant Offero entered, and for a while felt well content. But as it chanced, one day the court minstrel, in reciting a long poem, mentioned several times the Devil; and each time the Devil was named, the king crossed himself in self-defence. It was clear, therefore, that the king feared the Devil; and the giant accordingly forsook the king to enter the service of this mightier master. Now you must know, my young friends, that whenever men *want* to go to the Devil, they quickly succeed.

In a little while, therefore, Offero was in this new employ, and fully satisfied. But one day, following in the Devil's retinue, they came to a cross standing at the parting of the roads; and at the sight of the cross the Devil shuddered, and turned aside. This seemed odd, and in answer to a straight question of the giant's, the Devil confessed he feared the power of Jesus Christ, who died upon the cross. Then, said Offero, I will henceforth serve Jesus Christ. But Jesus Christ is not to be found without proper guidance, and for a long time, the giant sought in vain. At last, in despair, he applied to a hermit for instructions. The hermit directed him to fast and pray. But Offero had never learnt how to pray, and fasting did not agree with his constitution. He asked, therefore, if there were no other way of finding Jesus Christ. Now this Offero was some twenty feet in height, and could easily wade through a deep river in a few strides. The hermit, therefore, bade him go and make himself useful; and suggested that he could employ

his exceptional size and strength in no
better way than by taking up his abode
beside some river, where there was neither
bridge nor ferry, in order to carry people
from bank to bank who wished to cross.
And the hermit declared that if he did this,
and kept on doing it, he would some day
find the Lord Jesus Christ. At such a spot
then the giant built him a hut, and made it
his life work to take up in his strong arms
people who wished to cross the river, and
to wade through the water with them.
And so the years rolled by.   But Offero
had not yet found Jesus Christ; perhaps
he had even forgotten all about Him.
Now one night, after the giant had turned
in, there came over the water the voice of a
child asking to be carried across.   It was
not pleasant to be waked out of one's first
sleep, and children had no business wanting to cross in the night hours.   But the
good giant, without one grumble, bestirred
himself, and waded over to the other side.
There he found a little boy.   He took him
in his arms—he was but a feather-weight—

and stepped into the water again. And then a wonderful thing happened. At every stride the giant took the child's weight increased, until it seemed to Offero that he would sink in mid-stream under the burden. "Oh!" groaned the giant, "surely I carry the world." "Nay," cried a voice in response, "not the world, but the world's Maker dost thou bear." And when, breathless and exhausted, the giant set down his burden, behold he was no longer a child, but a full-grown man, with a kingly face and a halo of glory crowning his head. And with a cry of joy Offero recognised that he had borne in his arms the Lord Jesus Christ. And there and then the giant's name was changed from Offero, which means "I carry," to Christoffero, which means "I carry Christ." And that is the story of the Lord's surprise visit to the man who was ever after known as St Christopher.

You will have no difficulty, I think, in seeing what is the truth, the very beautiful truth, lying at the heart of this story.

Some of you would like, ah! so much, to see the Lord Jesus Christ, to hear His voice, to catch one of His sweet smiles. Dear young people, it is quite possible. Make it your daily business to be true and kind, and helpful and unselfish; be ready to offer your ungrudging service, even when it seems unreasonable it should be required, and some day the Lord will pay you a surprise visit. He may come in a very strange guise, but you will feel sure afterwards He did come. It may be as some half-crippled man wanting a strong arm to lead him across the busy street with its ceaseless traffic; it may be as a poor woman whose cart has been tipped over, and her wares are rolling along the ground; it may be as some little ragged urchin howling on the pavement, not much hurt, but very much frightened by his sudden tumble. If you are a St Christopher, the need of help will at once arrest you. And if you give it, what does our Lord Himself say? "Inasmuch as ye did it unto one of the least of these My brethren, ye did it

UNTO ME." Yes, yes. And you will feel,
ah! and see and hear that that is so too.
Do you say, But the cripple, the apple-
woman, the ragged boy will not really be
transformed into a true Christ-king with a
glory round His head, will they? I don't
mean exactly that; but I do mean this,
many of us have seen in the sweet smile of
some of the least of the Lord's brethren,
whom we have tried to help, something
more than earthly beauty, and in the "God
bless you, sir," or "Thank you kindly, dear
lady," we felt that something more than
a human voice spoke. We realised, in fact,
that the Lord had paid us a surprise visit,
and we went on our way rejoicing.

But remember, if you are to find these
happy surprises, kindness, thoughtfulness,
unselfishness will have to become your
habit. It will not do to be spasmodically
good-natured; like St Christopher, you must
daily be looking out to see what services
you can render. I want to drive this lesson
deep home, because your own happiness in
this life, and your reward in the life to

come, depend greatly upon it. And so I reproduce the story and its moral in another form for you, and in such a form as I hope may cause it to stick fast in your minds.

THE LEGEND OF ST CHRISTOPHER.

ONE hundred years had scarcely gone,
When in the land Christ smiled upon,
The giant Offero outshone
The mightiest heroes of his day,
And proudly proffered to obey
The man no higher power could sway.

Forth journeying, he thus became
Servant to one whose widespread fame
No mightier monarch's put to shame.
But when at court the minstrel's rhyme
Laid to the Devil some foul crime,
Lo ! the king crossed himself each time.

"How then !" quoth Offero, "art thou
Afraid of Satan ?   Sire, I vow
Satan shall be my master now."
Alas ! one day the Devil spied
A wayside cross, and vainly tried
To pass, then shuddering turned aside.

"Ho !" cried the giant, "by whose power
Art thou forced back ?" and from that hour
He sought the Devil's conqueror.
"Go fast and pray," a hermit said.
The giant begged a task instead,
"Then dwell beside some torrent-bed."

Now dwelling thus, the giant bore,
For months and years, each traveller o'er
Across the flood from shore to shore.
One night a child his aid besought ;
Behold ! mid-stream a marvel wrought,
The world to this child's weight were nought !

"Yea," cried a voice, O sweet and rare,
"For the world's Maker thou dost bear ;
Be, Offero, henceforth Christopher."
And lo ! fast held in his embrace
A radiant form, whose kingly face
Shone with a smile of heavenly grace !

Blest truth ! with legend intertwined,
By patient toil to serve mankind,
Our long-sought Lord Himself we find.
And, lowly though the labour be,
A sweet voice answers graciously,
"Ye did the service unto Me."

Sea=urchins and Sea=anemones.

"Be kindly affectioned one to another."—ROM.
xii. 10.

I WAS at the sea-side the other day, and as I wandered by the shore I took special notice of two very different creatures, as unlike as possible in shape, size, and form ; but they had one thing in common, both said as plainly as could be, "Don't touch me." The one creature was contained within a hard globe-shaped shell, covered completely over with sharp spines, and every spine cried out, "Don't touch me, or I'll hurt you." I did touch one. I put my arm down into the water, and grasped it, and lifted it out, and it did hurt me with those sharp spines. Many of you will guess at once that this creature was what is commonly called a sea-urchin. You will find them in many sea-side places, if you are careful to look at the extreme low-water mark. The other creature I found in a little fairy-like pool amongst the rocks. It was a thick red stalk crowned with a beautiful flower-like disc, and the lovely tentacles were gently moving to and fro like the petals of a chrysanthemum. You will guess again that I mean the so-called sea-anemone. Well, this little creature also cries out, "Don't touch me, or I'll hide all my beauty." I touched one, and immediately the tentacles were curled up and tucked away in the body, and nothing remained but a little red gelatinous lump stuck to the rock.

Now haven't you often seen boys and girls behaving in a similar fashion—especially at play? Because it is in your play hours, my young friends, that your real character most of all shows up. At home you are under restraint, at school you are under discipline; but in your spare hours, when you are giving yourself up to fun, and frolic, and games, it will soon be seen how far you are under self-control, and to what extent you are seeking and obtaining that grace of the Lord Jesus Christ, which will make you unselfish in your play as well as industrious in your work. Now here is a lad, for instance, who always wants to have his own way, and if he cannot get it he is as disagreeable and quarrelsome as possible, and makes everybody about him uncomfortable. He throws out angry words, perhaps even comes to blows. You must not thwart him in any least thing, or you will find out at once that he is a spinous creature like the sea-urchin, and his rough unkind words will give pain. Here is another lad, who will not get into a bad temper and grow violent, but if he cannot have all his own way he says he won't play. All his smiles and cheerfulness are gone, and, like the sea-anemone, he hides all the beauty of his character the moment you touch him. It is always a temptation to young people, and to a great many older folk too, either to grow angry or sulky when they cannot have their own way.

But listen to what the Apostle Paul says, "Be kindly affectioned one to another." This belongs to the fine shading in of Christian character, but its beauty and lovableness, and influence for good, depend a great deal upon it. I daresay you have often looked at the amateur work of some young would-be artist. There are the cliffs and the trees, and the shore and the sea; you can make out every feature of the picture quite clearly; but yet the whole is painfully crude, and you can tell at a glance what an immense difference there is between this early effort and the finished landscape of a practised painter. But where does the difference come in? It is in the management of light and shade, in subtle half-tones, in skilful perspective. It is something like this in the making of Christian character. Without justice and

K

truth and righteousness you cannot be
followers of Jesus Christ at all; but if you
are to have a finished and beautiful character, you must be careful to fill in some
further virtues, of which kindly affection is
one of the most important. There is many
a lad who would think it wrong to deceive
his parents, or disobey his schoolmaster,
who thinks nothing of grieving a companion by an unkind word, or spreading
gloom at home by going into the sulks for
half a day. And so his life is like a badly
painted picture, of which people say it's
not amiss for an early attempt, but no one
would care to have framed and hung up
in the house.

I want you, dear young folk, to carry
your religion into everything. Don't let it
be a matter only of going to Sunday
school, and listening to preachers, and
singing hymns in God's house. Take it
into your home duties, and your school
lessons, and into your play. If I had to
choose a lad for some important position, I
don't think I should inquire how he passed

his examinations, or what his behaviour was at table. I should go to the cricket-field, and watch him in the playground, and if I saw that in his games he was considerate and unselfish, full of zest and eagerness in the game, but always thoughtful for the interests of those playing with him, I should say that is the lad to take, and I should feel sure of his growing up into a fine man.

It would have been very delightful if there had been given us in the Gospels a glimpse of the boy Jesus at play. In certain writings, known as the Spurious Gospels, we have an imaginary portrait of Him, and a very bad portrait it is. It represents Him as using His miraculous powers to injure the lads who in any way crossed Him. We may be perfectly certain, however, that when, as a boy, Jesus joined with the other village lads at Nazareth, He was known and loved by them all as the fairest, and kindest, and best-tempered boy in that little town, and in all their games and excursions no one would be so popular and welcome as Mary's son. So much as that indeed is actually recorded, for St Luke expressly states that " Jesus increased in wisdom and stature, and in favour with God and man."

Let the boy Jesus be your example, and when you are tempted to be prickly-tempered or sulky-tempered pray for grace to overcome your faults. Don't be like sea-urchins or sea-anemones, saying in effect to every one, " Don't touch me," but be instead so kindly affectioned that all your companions may be able to rely upon it that you at least will not be quick to take offence. And if you thus copy Jesus Christ, it will be with you as it was with Him, you also will "grow in favour with God and man."

Playing the Man, or The Moral of a Coin.

"Quit you like men."—1 COR. xvi. 13.

DO you know, my young friends, that wherever English gold circulates it bears a marvellous and beautiful story? Every sovereign coined in recent years has a sermon to preach to those who have ears to hear, and the text of the sermon is, "Resist the devil." The next time you have a chance take a good look at a sovereign, or a crown-piece will do equally well. On one side you will notice the figure of a horseman. The horse is plunging wildly; the rider, his cloak flying back, and his sword firmly grasped, is about to strike a tremendous blow at a grim monster lying beneath the horse's hoofs. The horseman is the knight St George, and the monster a dreadful dragon. The story represented runs something like this. Once upon a time—it was very long ago—there was a city called Silene, on the north coast of Africa, and a dragon, a monster of enormous size and terrific aspect, and most voracious appetite, had taken up its abode in a swamp just outside the town. From this hiding-place the dragon used to sally forth, and waylaying the town people would drag them to its lair and devour them. The beast could not be tamed, and there was not a man in Silene brave enough to fight it. Soon the town was seized with a panic, and the question had to be faced what could be done to save the people from the dragon's rage, for unless something were done at once they would soon be all destroyed. And what do you think they decided to do? They decided to drive a bargain with the dragon, and give him

something to let them alone. First they
bargained to give the monster two sheep
every day, until, as you can easily imagine,
mutton became very dear in that market.
When the sheep were exhausted they
offered one man a day instead. I suppose
they would begin by feeding the dragon
with all the rogues and vagabonds, and
cripples, and fools, the town contained,
until there were only soldiers and honest
capable citizens left. When it came to
giving these they had to change the bargain
again, or the town would soon have
become defenceless. And then they sent
to the dragon each day a young girl.
The girls were chosen by lot, and one day
the lot fell upon the king's daughter.
There was no escape for her. She went
forth, dressed in bridal costume, and as she
went she wept and bemoaned her sad fate.
Now just at that time the great knight
St George came by, and when he heard
the cause of the lady's tears he undertook
to fight the dragon. It was a terrible
combat, but at last the knight slew the

monster and delivered the princess and the city.

From this curious old story many a lesson has been drawn, but there is just one point I want you particularly to notice. It is this : St George only did what any man in Silene might have done long before if *only he had had the courage!* Think what an awful loss there had been in sheep and men and girls, all for want of a little courage. The people tried to buy the monster off, and it had to be fought and slain in the end. What a pity there was no brave St George amongst them to fight and slay it at the beginning.

And now I think you will see what I want you to learn from this legend. You have each one of you to fight the dragon Sin. Do not, my dear young friends, make the terrible mistake of trying to buy off sin, instead of courageously facing and overcoming it. Many a man has made that blunder, and what has been the result? Sin has taken from him first character, then friends, then money, then health, and in the end he has had to fight sin to escape destruction body and soul. Sin will come to you in different forms, besetting some of you in the form of bad temper, and others in the form of deceit, and others in the form of selfishness, and so on. But in whatever form it attacks you, make a brave stand against it from the first.

Sometimes I hear a boy say, " I can't help getting cross." But, dear lads, you must help it, or from getting cross about little things you will go on to getting angry about more serious matters, and some day the dragon Anger may destroy you. Or I hear a girl say, " I can't help telling fibs. It's so hard to tell the truth sometimes." But, my poor girl, hard though it be you must do it, or from telling fibs, as you call it, you will go on to habitual falsehood, and some day the dragon Untruth may destroy you. You must deal with these dragons, dear children, as a certain pony I once knew had to be dealt with. He was a headstrong and mischievous, but very knowing animal. As soon as any stranger went into the field where he grazed, Tommy rushed at him, head down and heels up. If the stranger showed the slightest fear, Tommy would drive him right out of the field. But if the stranger went straight up to Tommy without flinching, and spoke sharply, and gave him a ringing smack on the flanks, Tommy was as quiet as a lamb and would submit to anything. You must deal so with your sins. Go right up to them, and smite them in God's name, and the victory will be yours. But remember, if instead of playing the man you play the coward, sin will take from you first one thing and then another, until it has stripped you of all that makes life worth living.

And now, in order to put this story and its moral in the briefest possible compass, I am going to cast it for you in verse. You can easily commit the verses to memory, and whenever you are tempted they will remind you that you are " to play the man."

THE LEGEND OF ST GEORGE AND
THE DRAGON.

WHAT means this strange device and bold,
A tale in sculptured figures told,
On England's world-strewn discs of gold?
This knight, hard pressed, who scorns to fly?
This wounded monster loth to die
Raging in mortal agony?

This is the beast of ancient fame,
Silene's bitter curse and shame,
Whom none durst fight, and none could tame!
Tribute the people paid him there
In sheep and men, then in despair
Dragged tender virgins to his lair.

Daily the girls by lot were drawn
Alas! on one ill-fated morn
They drew their monarch's fairest born.
In bridal costume, richly dight,
Weeping she went, when lo! this knight
St George rode by and marked her plight.

"And why these tears?" quoth he, "fair maid?
Tears, and in bridal robes arrayed!"
And when he knew, forth flashed his blade,
Straight on the fearsome thing he flew;
Stout was his heart, his steel was true;
Ere night closed in the beast he slew!

Oh, for thy courage, dauntless knight !
Oh, for the cunning hand to smite
And slay the dragon Sin outright !
To yield means daily sacrifice,
And still we multiply the price,
And countless victims ne'er suffice.

Go through the world, bright English gold,
Bear far and wide this tale of old !
Bid men be strong and true and bold ;
Bid nations cease to buy off Sin ;
Daring and truth shall surely win,
And bring on earth God's kingdom in.

The Gold=fish and the Minnows.

"Unto every one of us is given grace."—
EPH. iv. 7.

I MET one of my young friends the other day in the street carrying with great care some article he had just purchased. It proved to be a glass jar filled with water, in which a gold-fish and three or four minnows were swimming about in a very lively fashion. I stopped to look and admire, and as I looked I seemed to acquire the power, which certain people in olden-time tales were fabled to have, of understanding the language of beasts, birds, and fishes. The gold-fish seemed to be saying, as he swam to and fro with steady deliberate strokes of his fins, "Just look at me, see what a fine fellow I am with my rich golden colouring. Was there ever anything more beautiful than a gold-fish?" But the minnows were darting about with rapid movements of restless dissatisfaction, and they seemed to be complaining, "Why are we such plain little things, with never one golden scale to boast of! It isn't fair."

And so I began thinking. Now the gold-fish *was* beautiful. His gleaming scales flashed magnificently in the brilliant sunshine,—*but* he had a somewhat ugly bull-like head and a thick-set figure. And the minnows were sober-coloured compared to him. But after all, what beauty of form was theirs, and what exquisite movements! And then there came into my mind that comforting reflection the Apostle Paul suggested to the good people at Ephesus, "Unto every one of us is grace given." Yes. Even here, in the jar of fish this lad held in his hand, the great law of compensation was carried out. To the gold-fish was given grace of colour, to the minnows grace of form and motion.

There are two words, my young friends, in this text upon which I want you to lay stress. First of all read the passage in this manner, " Unto EVERY ONE of us is grace given." That is to say, upon *every one* of us is some favour bestowed. Some of you, like the minnows, may be without those conspicuous talents which attract general attention and admiration. But you will not be without grace of some kind. I used to know a dear old lady in a Berkshire village who was poor and plain and blind. But her face, when it lit up with a smile of contentment, as it always did at the mention of God's goodness, had a peculiar charm. To her was given the grace of helpfulness. She would wander from cottage to cottage, feeling her way with her stick, and wherever there was sickness or sorrow she would enter in and speak words of comfort and encouragement. And many a faint heart was made brave by her message of sympathy and hope.

I knew a girl in another southern village who was a humpback, in size a dwarf, and dreadfully deformed. For a while she was very bitter in spirit. She said God had made her different to every one else, and she had nothing to thank Him for. But to her also was given grace, the sweet grace of charity. There was just one thing she found she could do. She would wander far and wide through the meadows gathering beautiful wild flowers, and these she weaved into crosses and wreaths, and whenever there was a pauper funeral she would lay upon the coffin of the poor creature, for whom there was no other token of love or respect, her gift of hedgerow blossoms. And in so doing God's grace beautified her own life. Remember, my young friends, however humble your life, however few your talents, there is not a boy or girl to whom God has not granted the favour of doing something, and being something, which will make your life useful and beautiful.

But now I want you to read the text in

another way, by laying all the stress upon
the last word thus, "Unto every one of us
is grace GIVEN." Some of you, I hope
many of you, will perhaps become famous.
Some of you boys may become strong and
successful, some of you girls lovely and
clever. But do not forget strength and
success, and beauty and cleverness, are all
given. You must never, therefore, boast of
these things, or, because you possess them,
look down upon and despise others who do
not possess them. And do not overlook
this, that though God has bestowed upon
you *five* talents, the *one* talent of some
humble person may in some circumstances
be worth more than all your five. There is
a familiar old tale told of a certain professor, who, whilst being rowed across a
ferry, questioned the boatman as to his
attainments. "Can you read Greek?" he
asked. "No." "Or Latin?" "No." "Do
you understand philosophy or science?"
"No." And the professor despised the
boatman as a miserably ignorant fellow.
But presently the boat sprung a leak, and

the water poured in fast. "Now," said the boatman, "can you swim?" "No." Then said he, "It will go hardly with you." And if the boatman had not got the professor on his back, and bravely struck out for the shore with him, all the professor's acquirements would have proved very vain indeed.

Let me beg you, my young friends, never to fall into the folly and sin of bragging about what God has given you. Two lads, Ted and Dick, were playing one day in the garden. Ted's father had given him a silver watch the week before for a birthday present, and Ted was boasting about it. "That's more than you've got," said he to Dick. The tears almost came into Dick's eyes, for he had no rich friends to give him such presents. But through the open window the conversation reached Ted's father as he sat writing at his desk, and he called the lads in. "Ted," said he, "where did you get your watch, did you buy it?" "No, father." "Did you work for it?" "No, father." "Where did you get it from?" "Why, you know, father you gave it me." Then said he, "If you neither bought it, nor worked for it, but only received it as a gift, and Dick had no one to give him such a present, you have nothing to boast about. Now, you lads," he continued, "both of you come to me to-morrow afternoon." When they came the next day Ted's father handed to Dick a small parcel. He opened it, and found inside a beautiful gold watch. "Take it, my boy," said the gentleman, "I want Ted to learn how easy it is to destroy the ground of his boasting, and I trust you will be too wise to follow his example."

Think of this little story when you are tempted to boast, and then turn to the first chapter of St Paul's First Epistle to the Corinthians and see what he has written in the twenty-seventh and following verses. No, whether God has given much or little, let us be humble. For humility is like the beautiful ivy, which climbs over old ruins hiding their defects and covering them with glory, and which growing up the walls of fine brand-new buildings softens their outlines and adds to them an unspeakable charm. So humility makes the man of many talents not only bearable but charming, and crowns the man of few talents with a glory in which we lose sight altogether of the poverty of his gifts.

And, in the last place, I would remind you that whilst God has made men differ greatly in the variety and nature of their gifts, in the matter of one supreme gift he has made them all alike. To rich man and peasant, to philosopher and fool, He has granted equally the gift of His Son. If we have taken that gift for our own, we shall never murmur at the lack of any others, and without that gift all others are worthless.

And now, dear young people, whatever you may be, gold-fish or minnows, be content. Upon *every one* of you God has bestowed some grace, and whatever grace you have it is all *given*. Take it as from God, and use it for Him, and your life will be joyous and beautiful.

The Body and the Members.

"All the body fitly framed and knit together through that which every joint supplieth." — EPH. iv. 16 (R.V.).

IN this portion of his letter to the people at Ephesus the Apostle Paul is describing what makes a Church. Now, have you ever asked yourselves where the word *Church* came from, and what it means? It is really the Greek word *Kyriakon*, shortened into the Scotch form, the most correct form, *Kyrk* or *Kirk*, and into the English (having come to us in a roundabout way) *Church*. The Greek word *Kyriakon* means simply God's House. But when we use the word *Church*, some-

times we mean the building, and sometimes the people who gather in the building.   In the Greek another word is used
for this second meaning, namely *Ecclesia*—
that is, a number of people who are called
forth.   At Athens the word *Ecclesia* meant
a legislative assembly of the citizens
summoned by the crier.   In this epistle
the same word is several times translated
Church, and in its widest meaning it signifies
that body of men and women and children
who have been called forth from darkness
into light, and from the bondage of sin
into the glorious liberty of God's children.
And you, my young friends, if you are
sincerely trying to follow the Lord Jesus
Christ, are a part of His Church.   I want
you to notice therefore what the apostle
has to say about the Church, and about
the responsibilities of those, young or old,
who profess to belong to it.

Now there are many people who have a
sort of hazy idea that the Church means
cathedrals and bishops, and sermons and
hymns and ordinances, and that sort of

thing. There is nothing about it in this chapter. What St Paul does insist upon is that the Church means service. Not services, but just simply service. That if you belong to the Church, you have certain work to do that nobody can do for you, and that you have to do it in such a way that it may fit in with the work being done by thousands of others. And to illustrate these two points the apostle compared the whole Church to the human body, and individual Christians to particular parts.

And, first of all, he says the well-being of the body depends upon each part doing its own proper work. And what a variety of parts there is! Nerve, muscle, flesh, skin, bone, connective tissue, glands, arteries, veins, and so on. And people seldom think how much they owe to some of the smallest, and least known parts, that day and night carry on their functions. Of course you say, if the heart or the lungs were diseased, or if an arm or a foot were lost, it would be a serious matter for the body. But there are far less conspicuous

organs which if they were to strike work
for an hour would fill the whole body
with distress.   For instance, in the corner
of the eye there is a little organ called the
lachrymal gland.   It is constantly secreting
and pouring moisture upon the eyeball,
and so preventing any friction between its
sensitive surface and the socket in which it
turns.   If these little glands were to stop
work but for a short time, intolerable pain
would be the result.   So again, in all the
joints a membrane secretes an oily substance known as the synovial fluid, whereby
the ball-and-socket arrangement of the
joints works with perfect ease.   If these
organs were to cease work, the whole body
would be racked with anguish.   Now mark,
all these different parts have not only to
appropriate from the blood the nourishment
they need for their own vitality, but over
and above that they have to supply something for the common good of the body.

And so it is in the Church.   Each member has not only to take that which will
supply his own spiritual life, but to *supply*

something for the good of the whole body.
And no members are so humble, or obscure,
as not to be able to contribute something
which no one else can supply for them.
You, dear young people, cannot supply
the wisdom and guidance and experience
which older members can bring; but there
is much you can do, and in every Church
a great deal depends upon the earnest life
of the young men and young women, and
boys and girls. You can supply the brightness and freshness, and energy of youth.
For I want you to remember, what many
people entirely overlook, that the question
you should be continually asking is, *not*
What am I receiving? but, What am I
supplying? Because if you are constantly
receiving what the Church has to give,—
counsel, instruction, encouragement, comfort, sympathy,—and are supplying nothing
in return, you are like those unfruitful vine
branches about which the Lord Jesus Christ
says the gardener prunes them off, since
they waste the energy of the vine and pro-
duce nothing.

But now, when each member of the body
is doing its own work, it must also be in
communication with every other member,
and that communication is through the
brain.   From every member of the body
one set of nerves stretch to the brain, and
another set of nerves stretch from the brain
to every member, and so a double system
of perpetual telegraphy is going on throughout the body, and all the members are
thus " knit together," or, as the word
signifies, work harmoniously.   Now suppose
some day you run a thorn in your left
hand.   Straightway the message is flashed
to the brain, and from the brain a message
is flashed along the nerves to your right
hand, and immediately it proceeds to give
relief to the injured member.   And so,
through Jesus Christ, all the members of
His Church are in touch.   And see how
this works.   Here is a poor widow.   Her
rent is nearly due, her cupboard almost
empty, and her health broken down ; she
doesn't know what to do, or where to look
for help.   But she has faith in one unfailing

refuge. So she tells God all about it in prayer. And here is a rich man, who believes that he is only God's steward, and who prays often that his money may be a means of doing good. He is thinking of the people in his neighbourhood who require help, and somehow or other that poor widow comes into his mind. He calls at her cottage, and after a few kind inquiries leaves her a five-pound note. And as soon as he has gone the good woman gets down upon her knees, and says, " I thank Thee, dear Lord. I knew it would come right. The gold and the silver, and the cattle on a thousand hills, are all Thine, and Thou hast sent Thy servant to help the poor and needy." So you see those two members were brought together at the right moment, because each was in communication with Jesus Christ the Head of the Church.

It is a grand thought this. If you, my young friends, are living by daily prayer in communion with God, you have a living union with God's people all through the world. Yes, and with God's people in heaven too. There is no guild like the guild of Jesus Christ; there is no brotherhood like the brotherhood of Jesus Christ; there is no family like the family of God; there is no assembly so grand as the Church which is the body of Christ. Find your place in it, dear young folk, and find your work in it, and your life will be both a happy and a useful one.

Table Vessels and Kitchen Ware.

"Vessels of gold and of silver, but also of wood and of earth."—2 TIM. ii. 20.

PAUL at Rome dwelt in the neighbourhood of a great house, the palace of the Cæsars. Upon the royal table were costly vessels of gold and silver, in the kitchens were common vessels of pot and wood. Now you can readily understand that these different kinds of vessels would differ very greatly in the treatment they received and in their length of days. Pot mugs and wooden bowls would not be placed before the emperor, and golden goblets and silver dishes would not be used as kitchen ware. Many of the gold and silver vessels would have been carefully preserved from generation to generation, but the common wood and earthenware vessels would often wear out or be broken, and the worn bowls and broken pieces would come in the end to the rubbish-heap. And you can readily understand also that the gold and silver would not keep company with common pots. It would never do for these beautiful and costly vessels to be tumbled about with kitchen ware. If that were allowed their glory would soon be dimmed, they would become dinted and battered, and some of the smaller ones might easily be lost, and even find themselves at last, black with tarnish, and twisted out of shape, mingling with the refuse of the rubbish-heap.

So the apostle says, that in God's great household, the Church, there are different kinds of character corresponding to these different classes of vessels. There are men and women and children of golden character, fit for God's use. And there are others whose character is base and mean, and who are unfit therefore for God's service. And in the next place Paul warns Timothy that if God's true children would preserve their beauty of character, and continue "meet for the Master's use," they must avoid familiar association with all who, though they profess to be of God's household, are not true disciples of the Lord Jesus Christ.

Now there are two lessons here which it is most important that you, my young friends, should learn very early in life. The first truth is indeed a sad one to teach you, and yet it is far better that you should be distinctly taught it, than that later on you should discover it for yourselves, at some time and in some way, perhaps, that might do you much harm. It is this: There are many people who profess to be religious who are not so really; they come to God's House, they have their name perhaps upon the Church roll, they come to the Lord's Table, and yet, to use

a common and curious phrase, they are
no better than they should be.   And very
often people have been offended, and left
the Church, or refused to come into it,
because of these vessels of wood and earth.
It is very absurd of people to take offence
at this.   Jesus Christ distinctly told His
disciples that, right to the end, the wheat
and tares would grow together.   And Paul
is repeating the same lesson, when he says
that "in a great house are vessels not only
of gold and of silver, but also of wood and
of earth ; and some to honour and some
to dishonour."   For the apostle does not
mean by gold and silver vessels men of
wealth and position, and by wooden and
earthenware vessels poor and humble
Christians.   He calls every true Christian,
however humble, gold or silver ; and every
unworthy and insincere member, however
exalted, a vessel of wood or earth.   So
that you must neither be surprised, nor
discouraged, when you find people in the
Church who are not fit for God's service.
And never be so foolish as to say, when

you make such discoveries, " I won't stop
in such a Church any longer." Would it
not be very absurd of that beautiful golden
cup that many a time had stood on the
table at the king's right hand to say,
" Why ! I always thought all the vessels in
this household were pure gold, or at least
silver. I never thought there were common
pots in the place. I won't stay in this
palace a day longer !" Yet there are people
who act just as absurdly. Because they
find some inconsistent people in a Church
they leave it in disgust and go to another,
only to find more of these wooden and
earthen vessels there, and in every other
Church they try. It is very stupid of such
people, because they never will find a
perfect Church, and if they did they themselves would be refused admission. No,
my young friends, when you discover such
cases, don't be so foolish as that, but
resolve, by God's grace, to let the gold and
silver of your own character shine more
brightly.

But I would not have you go spying all

M

round to find out who are vessels of wood and earth. Let the great question with you be, Am I myself a vessel of gold or silver? And remember, it is not a question of size or shape, but of material. You may be sincere Christians, though small ones,—small in mind, body, and estate. The silver saltspoon is but a small thing, but it is a table vessel; whilst the great earthen bowl, vastly bigger and more conspicuous, belongs only to the kitchen ware. And so I want you to remember that some of the poorest and humblest, and least gifted members of the Church, are true gold and silver, and vessels "to honour." The Lord Jesus Christ has thousands of boys and girls in the world who are table vessels of precious metal. He is using them in His service, and they are happy in His favour. Are you, my dear young friends, amongst the number?

If you are, then let me impress upon you the second lesson. If you would keep the beauty and purity of your character, you must avoid evil companionships with vessels " to dishonour." I don't mean that you are to say to your schoolfellows, " I'm too good to play with you," or to the young people in business with you, " You can't have my company, you are not good enough." The Lord Jesus Christ treated the worst sinners with kindness, and we must try to be like Him. But don't choose for your close friends such as by their conversation and want of principle you find to be vessels of wood and earth. In all your necessary dealings with them remember this same apostle's rule, " Be courteous ;" but don't go running after them ; don't encourage their friendship ; let them clearly understand that if they would be your intimate friends, they must take your best friend, Jesus Christ, for their best friend also. How many men and women there are to-day, battered and tarnished vessels, who might have been living happy and noble lives, but for foolish friendships formed in boyhood and girlhood. And when the once beautiful vessels have been knocked out of shape, and have lost their lustre, there is only one remedy, they must go into the melting-pot, and be melted down and made over afresh. But what a pity it would be that you, my young friends, should lose the beauty of your character, and become so unfit for Jesus Christ's service through evil companionship, that nothing but a fiery discipline of sorrow could make you again " meet for the Master's use." Choose, first of all, Jesus Christ for your friend ; you will then be vessels of gold and silver. Choose next only those who love Jesus Christ ; and you will become more and more all through your life " vessels unto honour, sanctified, and meet for the Master's use, and prepared unto every good work."

The Story of Two Caterpillars.

"Flee youthful lusts."—2 TIM. ii. 22.

PUTTING this text into everyday language it would read, "Shun the desires natural to young people." I want to remind you, my young friends, that there are many temptations which older people with their experience of life are not likely to fall into, but by which you may very easily be beset and overcome. And some of those desires natural to youth seem so harmless, you can hardly believe any serious mischief will come of them. To help you to remember what terrible results may arise from small

and seemingly innocent things, I am going
first of all to tell you a little story, and
then in a few words I will try to make its
meaning plain.

On a beautiful bright summer morning
two caterpillars were feeding side by side
on the leaf of a lilac tree. They were very
young,—indeed they had not come out
from their eggs more than a few hours,—and
as they nibbled away at the juicy leaf they
were talking in caterpillar fashion of the
wonderful world in which they found themselves. Hovering near was a small fly. It
was an insignificant little thing, but it
seemed to regard the caterpillars with
friendly interest, and one of them felt
flattered. "Brother," exclaimed the other,
"beware! that little fly means mischief."
"Nay," replied the caterpillar, "what harm
can she do? She is but a merry little
thing, full of fun and frolic; she will be a
pleasant companion." But the other caterpillar, in alarm, crawled on to the next leaf,
and seizing its edge he fixed to it threads
of silk and curled the leaf into a roll, within

which he lay concealed. Now the little fly was in truth an ichneumon-fly, and under all her pretended friendliness she had a deadly purpose. She came near to the caterpillar that crawled unprotected upon the leaf, and settling close to it she thrust a sharp weapon into its soft body. The weapon was in fact a very minute gouge or tube, and through this the little fly deposited her eggs within the caterpillar's tissues. Then she flew away, laughing to herself. In a little while this caterpillar also, never supposing that a small fly could do any harm, but terribly afraid lest some bird should devour him, rolled a leaf about him and fed securely within its folds. In due time each of the caterpillars, having lived the extent of its caterpillar life, manufactured a horny case, and lay still within it awaiting its mysterious change into a winged moth.

Now one day two lads passed the lilac tree. They were brothers, and they spent nearly all their holiday afternoons seeking for caterpillars and butterflies, and bird's eggs, and newts and tadpoles, and all such things. "See!" cried George, "there is a leaf-roller here." "And here is another," cried Jack, "close to it." They unrolled the leaves, and in each one they found a chrysalis. "Let us take them home," said George, "and see which will come out first." So they carried the caterpillars, still fast asleep in their chrysalis state, home, and put each into a glass-covered box. A few weeks later, when George came down one morning, he went as usual to look at his chrysalis, and there lay the empty case, and near to it lay a pretty chocolate-coloured moth. He ran at once to call Jack. "Mine is out," he cried; "come along and let us look at yours." But to Jack's disappointment his chrysalis showed no change. But a few days later, to Jack's disgust, there issued from his chrysalis not a beautiful moth but a number of ugly look-ing little flies! This was a strange puzzle. The lads hurried away to their father to ask him about it. "Father," said George, "what do you think? Such a strange thing has happened. Jack's chrysalis is full of flies," and they showed him the box. "Ah, boys," said he, "I can explain this. A terrible fate has overtaken Jack's caterpillar. These are ichneumon-flies. Before this caterpillar became a chrysalis a fly like one of these had attacked it, and laid its eggs within its body, and there the eggs have hatched, and the little creatures have eaten up the caterpillar; and now that they have grown to full size, they have burst through the shell, and here they are instead of a beautiful moth like George's."

And now, my young friends, let me explain this little tale to you. It often happens that two brothers brought up in the same home, or two lads friends together at the same school, turn out very differently in later years. The one develops a beautiful character, full of goodness and truth and courage. The other instead disappoints everybody by developing only a brood of evil passions. How is it? It is because the one lad has drawn around him the protection of prayer and God's

Word, and the other has taken no care to guard himself, and so has become a victim to youthful desires,—youthful desires, that at the time seem little things, but which attack the soul with deadly effect. Let me mention a few of those desires natural to youth.

There is the desire of self-glorification, a longing to be praised. It is an evil desire, first because it will lead you to make too much of what people say about you, and too little of what God thinks of you. There were certain people whom Jesus Christ condemned because they loved the praise of men more than the praise of God. And next, it is an evil desire because it will lay you open at once to be ensnared by those people, and there are many such, who will seek to gain an advantage over you for their own ends by a little hollow flattery. Let your very first aim be to make sure at the close of each day that Jesus Christ can say of you, "Well done, good and faithful servant." If you have Jesus Christ's praise, you can do without

anybody else's ; and if other people praise
you too, their praise will be just and true,
and will only do you good. And you will
never then fall into that meanness of not
being able to endure hearing others praised
besides yourselves.

Another desire of youth is the desire of
being first. I was one day sitting next to
the driver on a coach when he pointed out
to me the front horse. "Do you see that
'oss, sir?" he said, "well, we always 'as to
make that 'oss leader. He won't pull in
the shafts." There are some boys and
girls, yes, and some of them of many years'
growth, like that horse. If they can't be
first, they won't do anything at all. That
also is an evil desire, and young people
who give way to it are sure to grow up into
disagreeable men and women.

Then there is the desire of always having
one's own way. How natural this is to
young people! There are so many things
that are expected of you that you don't
like to do, and you don't see any reason
for doing, lessons set you at school, duties

laid upon you at home. Dear young friends, as you value your future, submit to the love and wisdom of parents and teachers, and believe that your own way is often the worst way possible.

Or, once again, there is the desire of ease. There are hundreds of men and women to-day whose lives are wretched and useless because they never learned as boys and girls *to buckle to.* It was so easy to copy a sum from the next boy's slate, to translate a difficult passage of Greek or Latin by means of a key, to lay the burden of some unpleasant duty upon a younger brother or sister.

Shun all such evil desires. Let them get no hold upon you. Remember at home, at school, at play, God's eye is always on you, and if you flee these youthful desires, presently when you enter into your manhood and womanhood you will find yourselves endowed with powers and faculties that will make life very joyous to you ; and more than that, when later you have passed through the chrysalis stage of death, you will emerge into the glory of a blessed and eternal life!

So let this little tale dwell in your minds, and whenever you feel an evil desire coming near you think of the caterpillar and the ichneumon-fly, and instantly protect yourselves by prayer for God's help.

SOME OPINIONS of the PRESS

ON THE

"GOLDEN NAILS" SERIES.

"The outstanding feature of the Addresses is their simplicity and suitability for the minds and wants of the little ones for whom they were printed. The language is simple, the addresses are short, and the lessons taught are illustrated by suitable stories, without which the attention of the young cannot readily be sustained."—*Dundee Advertiser*.

"Will delight those whose life is yet all before them ; and more, will aid, pleasantly and quietly and surely, in forming that groundwork of preparedness which goes so far to make life worth living."—*Liverpool Post*.

"Conveying lessons of wisdom, kindness, and humility so attractively, that boys and girls, and their elders too, will read with delight and profit."—*Pray and Trust*.

"Well planned, simple in language, pointed, and filled with apt and telling illustrations."—*North British Daily Mail*.

"Every volume has had a good reception, and every new volume increases one's admiration for the enterprise. We have always felt that if three things were made imperative—freshness, truth, and cheapness—there was a great field for children's sermons, for we knew that there were children and children's preachers who were hungering and thirsting after them as after righteousness itself. The latest volume of the 'Golden Nails' Series is as happy as its happy title. It is worthy of its place."—*Expository Times*.

"Written in a bright, easy, and popular style, and the sound, practical advice that they give is appropriately illustrated by a copious supply of anecdotes drawn from history. Children should read them with interest."—*Scotsman*.

"Models of brevity, clearness, and attractiveness."—*Kilmarnock Standard*.

"Characterised by simplicity of diction, suitable illustration, and commendable brevity." — *Hamilton Advertiser*.

SOME OPINIONS of the PRESS

ON THE

"GOLDEN NAILS" SERIES.

" Should prove a boon to Sabbath School teachers."— *Hawick Advertiser.*

" A worthy addition to a list of bright and interesting addresses or sermonettes to children. The language is simple, and the illustrations being drawn from everyday life, bring the lessons easily within the grasp of quite young children."—*S.S. Chronicle.*

" Simple, practical, and pointed, neither a ' taking down ' nor a ' strain up.' "—*Christian Leader.*

" The addresses are admirably suited to their audience. The style is simple, the divisions are felicitous, and the teachings are wholesome and practical." — *Glasgow Herald.*

" Containing twenty lovely addresses, in each of which a father's heart tenderly yearns over the children to whom he thus speaks. The stories, which form a prominent feature in the most successful of such sermons, are well chosen, and not by any means of an antiquated type, and parent, preacher, and teacher may read with pleasure and profit."—*Methodist Recorder.*

" These addresses can be heartily commended, for they are sure to exercise a healthy influence upon the minds of juvenile readers. Not only are the thoughts and sentiments unexceptional, but they are clothed in graceful and impressive language."—*Dundee Courier.*

" The sermons are such as children can understand and value. The language is plain and direct, and not a few incidents related are new in the connections in which they are found. It is a wholesome book."—*Youth.*

" An admirable collection, which has done so much to popularise sermons and addresses specially intended for the young. The truths enforced are presented in a most attractive manner."—*Christian Commonwealth.*